THE INVISIBLE WAR

Unveiling the Secret World of Spiritual Warfare

JOE CETRONE

Tate Publishing, LLC

ISBN: 1-59886-04-8-8

*This book is dedicated to all
the lost souls who seek the answer.*

CONTENTS

PREFACE

If we were to view the world on a spiritual level, I could guarantee one thing. By the time, we thought we might have figured out an answer, someone would have come up with another more fitting. The problem is that man has no limitations or restrictions to his thought capacity. Every mind is completely different from another, which can give us a creativity that knows no bounds.

Being a created life that has intelligence is a blessing all of its own, but there is so much more to it than meets the eye. We are so in tune to what we can see and touch that we tend to forget what we see, or for that matter—cannot see. Everyone has a fear of the unknown—not knowing what lies ahead in the future, or better yet, not knowing what is in store for us. At one time or another, I'm sure we all have lain in bed and thought about getting old or passing away. However, we always seem to somehow put it aside and go to sleep, and everything becomes fine in the morning. Did you ever ask yourself why?

The reason our thoughts become more fearful at night is that we lie in darkness with things we cannot see—only thoughts passing—with no visual aid from the human eye. It is almost safe to say our fears come from darkness, and yet it also can be a security blanket in which we hide. We feel that we can get away with almost anything if we can hide ourselves. Darkness almost becomes a haven for us, while it can also hold our biggest fears in life. Light on the other hand, gives us a clearer picture, a sense of warm comfort. It's funny, but in reality and on television as well, you will notice that arson, thefts, and homicides always seem to happen at night, inside the darkness. Another statistic is that most criminals are caught in the daytime. That is because darkness cannot comprehend light. The two are opposite. Our eyes are always open and able to see most things in the light. If you were to sit in a dark room and turn the light on, you would completely wipe out darkness. Even if half the room is dark, the half that is lit up dominates its own side. The same would follow if we were to talk about black and white or good and evil. The two cannot dwell in the same place, but they can occupy their own environments in different parts of a sequence.

I pondered so many thoughts that referred to dark and light in all different facets. The only conclusion I could find was that the two ruled in their own established worlds, dominating only where allowed to reign. In the spiritual world, the two are very much active and needed to put forth what the overall plan will be for our lives. There are always three sides to every story: yours, mine, and the truth. The point is that we always choose a side. We are either for or against some opposing force. In the end, like in all things, there is a winner and a loser, a right or wrong, a good or bad. In the spirit world, it works very much the same. To speak universally, we would have to say there is a force of darkness and a force of light. The sun is the only source that separates night and day.

There is a whole other world that we cannot see, a world that holds its own light and darkness—a world that is invisible to the eye unless light can shed itself upon each one of us. We are going to discuss a few things in this book and take them to another level without sounding religious. There are levels that we can all relate to in this never-ending battle of confusion. Let us all prepare together to enter into the *Invisible War.* I hope to better your understanding of how things that we cannot see may affect our lives and alter what we do today and for the future to come.

(1)
OUT OF DARKNESS INTO LIGHT

I was raised a strong Catholic, growing up in the city of Providence, Rhode Island. Before relocating and moving to the suburbs, I went to school there until I was eight years old. I had so many questions about life with so few answers. I felt I always had an understanding about spirituality. I was always creative in finding things to do to occupy myself, spending much of my time thinking and being very imaginative. My thoughts of fantasy and reality were not so far apart. I could always amuse myself with the smallest and meaningless things and found happiness in doing them.

I had always believed in God, but never had enough understanding of who He really was. I knew Him in the knowledge of what people taught me and just filled in the rest of the blanks myself. It didn't mean that I was right, but I felt that my interpretation of God gave Him more life than what I was hearing and also learning. I started to become interested in God and the supernatural at the age of six. I remember sitting in church during a Sunday evening service, listening to the priest talk while looking above him at the huge Cross that had Jesus hanging upon it. I watched people praying and touching it, as if it were real. I began to stare all around at these figures of worship. Believe me when I tell you, I started to become frightened. I did not see God in the way that I was being shown. I pictured Him a warm and gentle Spirit who we could not see, while others seemed to believe that He was in all those figures hanging up at the altar.

Time went on, and I started developing different interests as a child. I was into playing with my friends a lot. We would cause trouble and stay out as late as we could. I do not think I ever forgot God, but I didn't have enough depth of Him to stay in focus. I asked questions that no one ever seemed to answer in the way I needed to hear. I would always get, "That's the mystery of the church. One day you will understand." Therefore, I went on believing things the only way I knew how. Eventually, I lost interest and started getting into hobbies, like drawing, putting together monster models, and playing with hot wheels. If it took being creative and using my imagination, then I was into it.

Music was a big part of my family. Almost everyone on my Dad's side played an instrument. While growing up, my Father supported us by playing out four to five nights a week in a band. Back then, you could earn a living by performing music. My mom stayed home with my sister and me on those nights, and we would watch many movies. Horror was our top choice. I enjoyed scary movies very much, and it became a custom in our household to watch them. They say that we learn to program everything in our minds at a young age. Well, for me, it was spirituality and horror movies. There was a time when we would go visit my mother's friend a few nights a week to hang out. I was scared to go in there. I don't remember much, being that I was six years old, but I do remember a few things that influenced me as a youth.

My mother's friend had a creepy looking house. I remember a lot of lit candles and weird pictures hanging up on the walls. The woman was nice to my sister and me, but after a while, I wanted no part of her. I could go deeper into the story, but out of respect to certain parties, I won't. The woman was a witch who practiced Satanism. Tarot cards and séances were not out of the ordinary for her. I found myself drawing pictures of the devil in first grade. Images that I would see in books or in movies influenced my thoughts every day. I had become very intrigued by the supernatural that it controlled most of my thinking. While other children occupied their time playing with G.I. Joe dolls, I was trying to understand the forces of darkness. I did have a normal lifestyle in the physical world, but when it came to my thinking, it was complicated, and I was a mess.

Years passed by and my life became an average one. I played sports and dated women, but I always felt that I was missing something. I ended up finding my musical talent at about ten years old. It was none other than the drums. I listened to bands like Kiss and Black Sabbath to soothe my mind. I never really had to practice music. I had the talent inside of me. I would only have to practice exercises for the physical part of playing, because I was born with natural rhythm. I started lifting weights and looking good. Ego was everything to me. I felt so far advanced in a lot of ways that common sense became difficult for me.

I then hit my teen years, where I was ready to explore—sex being the first on my mind. I also started smoking pot and hanging around with the tough crowd. By the time I had hit seventeen, I was experienced in many ways. I started rehearsing with a band that was getting ready to play out and make some money. Still, I was searching for that something to make me tick. I seemed to become bored with things so easily that I always needed to be stimulated to keep focused. I then reverted to what I knew best, the dark side.

I found myself tapping into the occult and hanging around with strange people. I knew deep down that I never gave myself totally to the dark side. I mean I always thought about God, but power, lust, and greed made God and religions seem very weak. I then fulfilled all the lust-filled pleasures that I could think of. There were not many fleshly desires that I did not accomplished in my day. I still knew deep down that it was wrong, but desire ruled my flesh.

I then hit my twenties. I started playing out in clubs and having relationships with women. I don't think I ever wanted a relationship to the point of being married; I just had them for the sake of saying I'm in one. The truth was that I probably created havoc for myself basing all my relationships on sex. I feel we rebound in and out of relationships because we do not want to face the hurt from a prior one. Therefore, we bounce everywhere to fill the emptiness that we carry. Unfortunately, nobody wins. Someone always gets hurt. Children suffer at our expense and because of our own selfishness. Therefore, time went on, and I was faced with a tough decision. The person whom I was dating became pregnant. I knew that it was wrong to have an abortion, but I was not ready to become a father. I still wanted to hang out with my friends and play in a band. I made the best of it. I forced myself to become a family man.

The whole problem with me was that I still needed to find that peace inside that made me happy. I really thought it was music. I loved being in the spotlight and watching people enjoy my drum playing. I knew that once I had taken the stage, it was only a matter of seconds before I would capture someone's attention. I felt confident knowing that women were drawn to by my looks and ability to put out a sound that was original. See, I took gifts that some people wish they could have and twisted them up to suit my personal needs. A creative mind and musical talents would have carried me a long way, if it were not for my vanity and pride.

One day I ran into my old friend, Chris, at Super Stop and Shop. I had not seen him since high school. I remember envying him for having the biggest biceps. I took down his number, and we planned to get together and hang out. Chris and his wife ended up coming over that weekend, and we enjoyed some burgers and dogs on the grill. It was nice to laugh and hang out, forgetting life's problems for a few hours. I don't know how we got on the subject, but witchcraft came up in the conversation—something I never figured would take place. Chris then asked me if I had a Bible. The first thought from my mind was, *No, not one of those religious freaks.* I went into the bedroom and got him a Bible that was collecting dust, and he began to read from it.

The whole part about religion at that point of my life was something I didn't want to deal with. The funny part was that Chris showed me things in the Bible I never thought existed. There was a glow on his face when he spoke about God. It was intense. I watched goose bumps appear on his arms as he talked. I saw the inner peace he was feeling and wanted to feel the same. It was only a few hours shortly after that I accepted the Lord as my Savior.

I read, searched the Scriptures daily, and prayed continuously. We had Bible study at my house once a week. I finally found a warm and loving peace that seemed to have no limitation. The more we prayed, the more intense the feelings became. We introduced the Lord to family and friends, and it did not cost a dime or take much effort at all. For the first time, I honestly could say, "Life is great." I know it may sound strange, and I also know it's hard to believe, but trust me, there wasn't anything I could do that was more positive in my life at that point. It felt so right. I knew there was a light that shined over me that was incredibly overwhelming. I also knew there was a darkness that existed as well from my experiences.

Time went on, and I found myself arguing with my daughter's mother. It was not that she did not believe in the Lord. In fact, she also became saved. The problem was that I had a yearning that went deeper than hers did. I was still learning the basics, and we could not see eye to eye on things anymore. I knew about evil forces and something in my spirit told me that we were having problems due to being young Christians. It was apparent that the opposition (Satan) was not taking things lightly because of our decision in following Christ.

Being a true Christian is having a spiritual connection to God through the blood of Christ Jesus and the ability to have guidance by the Holy Spirit.

Once you tap into both sides, you will realize that good and bad dominate in the spirit world as well as here in the natural world. It was only a matter of time before I had lost my connection to God and turned to the "black arts" once again. This time, after receiving an even harder hit, I rebelled. I found myself separated from my future wife and daughter. I definitely believe beyond a shadow of doubt that our parting ways were due to us finding the Lord and not having enough depth to fix the problem. You should know one important thing; the enemy hates anyone who comes to the Lord. Once you do, you may realize life seemed better before you became a Christian.

A few months had past; I started a new job and met new friends. I began drinking and taking drugs again. I was working out heavily and going to strip clubs. I had affairs with women just to satisfy my desires of lust. My attitude changed completely along with my total mind set. I started to gamble on football games and sell drugs to make extra money. I totally went off the deep end. I will say this; while I did those things, I still felt the voice of God tugging at my heart. It wasn't strong enough to sway me in the right direction; I was too far gone. It was only a matter of time before I felt something drastic was about to happen. I felt evil take control over me like a plague. I even had a woman whom I dated for a while give me a nickname, "Dark One," because my heart was so cold.

As more time passed, I developed yet another gift, writing. It just came natural to me. I always had a desire to create what my mind thought of, but never knew how to project it. I was finally able to take a scene from my memory and paint a picture of a thousand words. I, of course, picked the supernatural. Deep down inside, my heart was genuine. I never wanted to be an evil person. I feel that there are two channels where evil can penetrate us:

1. Physical harm against someone else.
2. Corrupting your ideas with some imaginative thought that is not of the norm.

Either way, it traps you from both sides, physically and mentally. The devil had convinced my mind that as long as I was not hurting anyone physically, I could justify evil as pure. Vampires, werewolves, and ghosts were what I loved to write about and watch on the movie screen. All I could seem to do was watch horror. Every movie I rented or bought was evil. That was my comfort zone. I didn't know any other way. I know I could have made it as an author who wrote horror stories. In fact, publishing proposals were offered to me for some of the stories I had put together and sent out! It seemed that every time I had completed a story, something inside said that it was wrong, so I would throw it away. Yet every time I would convince myself not to write those kinds of stories, I would end up having the desire to write them all over again.

The last phase to my nightmare of horror became very real. I found myself arrested and put in jail for dealing with drugs. My life came to a complete stop. All the things I had done and all the people I hurt along the way finally had their moment of gratification. When the prison bars closed and I was being sentenced, life seemed hopeless. I could not help but think of where I was a few years back. I was seeking God, feeling so peaceful, and now corrupted with filth and all alone.

One night while sitting in total darkness, I started evaluating my life. I then prayed to God for understanding. I knew this was my fault. There was no one to blame except for myself. I just wanted to know how and why. I had a cellmate who didn't know how to read so well. I would help him with letters he wrote to his girlfriend. I also noticed he had a Bible. I would read it from time to time. He would ask me questions about God, and I would help him the best way I knew how. I remember the night before he was to be transferred to another facility; he told me how scared he was. I was a bit nervous to tell him about Jesus. Suddenly, I felt the presence of God fill the room. I asked the man to pray with me and receive Jesus in his heart. A few minutes later, he did.

I eventually moved to another building. I was in a better place than where I was prior. Funny, but the people I became associated with, as well as the correctional officers on my floor, were all Christians. We would have Bible studies daily and seek the Lord continuously. I grew up and learned a lot of things. I strengthened my character and grew spiritually strong once again. On the night before my parole hearing, I sat up in bed and realized all that had happened to me was just a test. God delivered me from the life I had lived—from the time I sat in church as a little boy, until now as I grew older and wiser. God never left my side. I left His. I needed to be on both sides to really realize how the two worked and operated, meaning good and evil. I needed to understand what forgiveness meant. There were so many events took place throughout my life, which only could have come from God. I know He had his hand in my life all along. The next day the presence of God filled the room yet again, and I made parole with immediate release.

It has been nearly seven years since my life took a turn. The officers that were my superiors are now my best friends. We gathered once a week for prayer and study. I also ended up playing drums for a praise and worship team at my local church. I have dealt with struggles along the way, as most Christians could understand. In fact, you would not believe how the enemy tried preventing me from writing this story for you, which leads me to why I am here. One day the Holy Spirit spoke to my heart about writing a book about warfare that we face as Christians. I took all the knowledge I had in Scripture, as well as the battle I went through to get me to this point. I hope that the topics we discuss can help equip you in life's long race to the finish line. If I could be a light in the world for just one person who reads this, then my job is complete. The only thing I want to accomplish is to give back what God has given me, eternal life. Know you are not in this alone. Understand that it is not easy. The true way to get through this is by using the power of Jesus Christ. God said in Joel 2:25 (KJV), *"**I will restore to you the years that the locust hath eaten**." Meaning, God will give back what the enemy had taken away and bless us more abundantly. It's time to prepare for a battle that needs much equipping. May the Lord give you the wisdom to understand the invisible war that we face each and every minute of our lives.*

(2)
KNOWING YOUR ENEMY

Like any battle, we need to prepare for the opposition. The first step to knowing your enemies is finding out who they are and why they became your foes. Before the creation of man, God dwelt in the Heavens with his host of angels. One of God's creations was that which we know as Lucifer. The name Lucifer means "Light Bearer." His beauty was precious, as a stone. Lucifer was a chief musician that was responsible for wonderful music played before the Lord. If you were to read the passages in the Old Testament Book of Ezekiel, Chapter 28, you would notice three important things about our enemy. Let's take it from verses 12–14 and cover the basics that sum it up best for us. Verse 12 **"Full of wisdom, and perfect in beauty"** *(knowledge and appearance). Verse 13* **"Thy timbrels and thy pipes were created for thee in the day thou was created"** *(music). Verse 14* **"Thou was the anointed cherub that covers"** *(held a high position in the angelic realm). KJV*

It's funny, but when you break it all down into today's world, you realize that evil does, in fact, follow these sequences—intelligent people with an outward beauty and a talent to make themselves lots of money for all the wrong reasons. That does not apply to everyone, and we will touch ground on that later in the book. Just try keeping that in your mind for now. Lucifer then decided what God had appointed him with was not enough to satisfy his needs. So he tried to do one better, he rebelled against God. Angels were created with free wills of their own. Instead, He gave angels the same choice that we have, the ability to decide on their own.

Lucifer fell when pride was found in him. He decided that he wanted to be like God. In fact, he wanted to be higher! The Book of Isaiah (14:12–14), explains the fall of Lucifer. **"How you have fallen from heaven, O Lucifer, son of the morning. You have been cast down to the earth, you who once laid low the nations. You have said in your heart "I will ascend into heaven; I will raise my throne above the stars of God; I will sit on the mount of the congregation. I will ascend above the tops of the clouds; I will be like the most high."**

Seeing how Lucifer fell, you could tell that he filled himself with pride. Everything was "I." That statement is something we all can relate to at one time or another. We tend to put ourselves above all things, even God. Lucifer was then cast out of Heaven and sent here on earth to rule his own kingdom. Jesus says in the Book of Luke (10:18) **"I saw Satan fall like lightning from heaven."** It would be just like him not to be the only one to fall. He had to manipulate others to believe his story as well. So, with free will as their option, a third of the angels bought into his lie and took his side. You can find that passage in the Book of the Revelation according to Christ Jesus, in chapter 12, verse 4, where it states **"His tail swept a third of the stars out of the sky and flung them to earth."**

The fall of Lucifer signified a lot for us and started the battle between good and evil. He also

obtained followers as well. We call them "demons."
If you study certain names in the Hebrew and Greek
text, you will find the meanings of what each angel
signifies. The whole purpose for the enemy here on
earth was to create an army of his own, in hopes to one
day defeat God. Until then, it's a battle for souls, and
he will stop at nothing to achieve what he set forth to
accomplish. That's where the spiritual battle begins.
Whether you believe in God or not, it's all real and
happening right before your very eyes. In fact, by not
believing, you have made the devil's job much easier!
Now he just has to work on the believers, and that is
half the battle. As long as the skeptics remain skepti-
cal, the enemy will have the upper hand. That is why
warfare is so complex. I once heard Pastor Adrian
Rodgers on WARV 1590 Life Changing Radio say,
"If you can't find the devil in your life, it's because he
is walking right along beside you without you even
knowing about it." The greatest trick of the devil is
to convince you that he does not exist.

If God exists, and He does, you must also
believe in the devil. The two go hand in hand.

To single one out only gives our enemy more
power. All the devil does is walk around the earth with
his demons and try to destroy our lives. The Book
of 1 Peter (5:8) gives us a clear picture of how he
operates. **"Our adversary the devil walks around**
the earth as a roaring lion seeking whom he may
devour." *That's self-explanatory if you think about*
it. So how does he try to destroy our lives?

The enemy's soul purpose is to blind the
hearts of believers. If you are not a believer in the
Word of God, you have made the devil's task much
easier. We, as people, are all so very different. We

have certain buttons to push, so many weaknesses and temptations; the enemy has many ways to attack. In reality, the power Satan has is the power we give him. Of course, that is much easier to say than to apply to our everyday thinking. Even though Satan is an angelic being, he still is very dangerous to the world. Satan is referred to the "**Prince of the power of the air**" as said in the Book of Ephesians (2:2). The term "air" is that of the invisible heavenly realm that we can't see with our natural eyes. The devil has been also called the "**god of this age**" as stated in 2 Corinthians 4:4.

There's one thing you need to know before we end this chapter. Realize that though it seems our enemy appears to be all-knowing at times, he cannot read our minds, nor is he omnipresent. Meaning, he cannot be everywhere at once as God can. It is only by our actions that he can determine our weaknesses. Just because he can't be everywhere does not mean that he is not capable of finding out information. A third of the angels fell with him, and they spread throughout the earth with assigned missions to destroy our lives. Demons then take this information and report it to their master and chief—Satan. A passage in the Book of Ezekiel (28:3) says, "**No secret can be hidden from him.**" The Scripture is not saying that he is all knowing. It means that he has nurtured every sin man has struggled with. Remember, he was the first to fall before man, so he knows how temptation works.

I hope you have a better understanding of who our enemy is. We will now look and see how he operates in the next chapter, but first, I would like to share something that I have pondered for a long time. I say *not to put all your marbles in this theory, but some of you may find it interesting. One night I was doing some research and found something quite intriguing. Throughout the Bible, God has always used numbers and symbols to signify times and events. I was doing a study of my own and broke down some important words and numbers that related to the enemy and his regime.*

1. Devil
2. Dragon
3. Dagon (Philistine god worshiped in the Old Testament)
4. Destroyer
5. Death
6. Disease
7. Darkness
8. Deceit
9. Deception
10. Depression
11. Devious
12. Despise
13. Disobedience
14. Dishonor
15. Distress

I took these fifteen words related with negativity that were compatible to the forces of darkness. The letter "D" had been signified with all the above words as the beginning letter for each of the words. I did some research on the occult one day and found some interesting things. In Satanic covens, they use symbols and wear certain pendants around their neck. One of the symbols designed in the shape of the number 4. It had been said that this number stands for the four-crowned princes of hell: Satan, Lucifer, Belial, and Leviathan. All are biblical names, so some truth stands in the theory I have. Here's the funny part: As the number four symbolizes their completion, the letter "D" is also the fourth letter of the alphabet. The Bible is full of so much information to obtain that one could spend a lifetime and only scratch the surface of God's hidden codes.

Satan is not the hideous-looking creature we envision; He does not appear donning an ugly face with horns. If that were the case, we would see sin as ugly. The problem is that although we know sin is wrong, we do not always classify it as sin. Revenge and sexual immorality seem to be the more forgotten sins. We find ourselves either getting even with somebody in some way or satisfying our fleshly appetite.

God uses word pictures throughout the Bible to describe things. Each of His symbols holds a particular message that God is trying to get across to us. The devil's actions and cruelty are what made him ugly and hideous, not his appearance. Remember, he was perfect and beautiful, a force of spirit, not of flesh. The enemy deceives us by disguising himself as something more appealing. If he were to appear to us any other way, we would surely run in the opposite direction. In the Book of 2 Corinthians (11:14), states, **"And no wonder! For Satan himself is transformed into an angel of light.***"*

I hope this chapter gave you a better understanding of who our enemy is. There is so much more that we can learn about him. I would suggest you to take the time to learn more by studying and researching Scripture. I tried to give you a foundation, but I always say to revert back to God's Word for the answers you are looking for. The Holy Spirit will then guide you into the truth. If you are with me so far, say "Amen," and let us move on.

(3)
THE BATTLEFIELD

*When first entering the arena, you need to have your invitation card. You must be "born again." This assures your spot in the family of God and gives you access to the main event. You must declare whose side you're on so you will be identified by your fellow allies. When Jesus shed his blood on Calvary two thousand years ago, he dropped the A-bomb on Satan and his forces. Jesus said in John 3:3, "***Unless one is born again, he cannot enter the kingdom of heaven.***"* *Born again is not a religion or a cult of weird Christians as most people think. It is a command from God himself. To be on God's ultimate force, you must be able to understand the commands that are given. Picture yourself training for an elite force. You must be disciplined, knowledgeable, and armed with your weapon at all times. The first thing you need to do is sharpen your sword, the Bible. The only way to win is to know what the Word of God says.*

There are so many different denominations and religions that you can become caught up by heresy. I don't like comparing religion to God; the two are totally different. Religion is man made, while serving God is a relationship. I do not care what your religion is: Catholic, Baptist, Pentecostal . . . You must be "born again." When you are born as a child, you enter into a new world. When you become born again, you enter into a spiritual birth that makes you reborn. That is it! There is no other reason for its title.

When we receive Jesus into our hearts and confess that he is Lord over our lives, He accepts us as His child. We need to realize that the penalty for our sins is death. If Jesus paid the price by shedding his blood, it is only right that we acknowledge that He suffered for you and me. We will talk a great deal more about Jesus later on, but for now, we need to touch on a few other points.

One important reason for paying attention to Scripture carefully is to be ready for deception. That's the enemy's greatest trick. If we are not in line with God's Word, we find ourselves easily led astray. Satan is famous for twisting the Word of God around. David said in Psalm 56:5, "**All day long they twist my words.**" That is because no one knows the Word of God better than the devil. That's right! Satan knows the Word better than we do. The tempter tried to deceive Jesus in the desert in Matthew 4, when he quoted a passage from Psalm 91. It's not by works that we defeat the devil or by being a good person; that only edifies yourself. It is by every word that proceeds out of the mouth of God, as Jesus quoted back to Satan in the desert.

Spiritual warfare is like chemical and bio-logical warfare that takes place in your mind. Each Christian is like a city under attack and your mind is the battlefield. Unless you allow God to control your thought patterns, you are setting yourself up for destruction. It is like survival of the fittest in a playing field that you cannot see. The place where Jesus was crucified was called Golgotha. In translated Hebrew,

Golgotha means "Place of the skull." Our battle is not of a fleshly fight. It is so amazing how every word or term used in the Bible relates to our lives today. Our area of warfare is also in a place of the skull, our minds. We're going to take a look at a passage in the Book of Ephesians (6:12), then break it down and see how it works. **"For we do not wrestle against flesh and blood, but against principalities, against powers, against the rulers of the darkness of this age, against spiritual hosts of wickedness in heavenly places."** *KJV*

Let us now break this Scripture down as Paul talked about. Take a look at some of the key words.

1. Principalities
2. Powers
3. Rulers
4. Spiritual hosts of wickedness

This is a description of the satanic government in its correct order of rank, with of course, Satan as the commander and chief controlling it. This refers to the battle that we Christians have to contend with each day. It can be in conjunction with the angelic realm of evil that operates in the Heavens. Once each demon is assigned to a particular mission, then the orders can be carried out. First, you need to know how the Heavens operate. People seem to miss the three parts of Heaven in the Bible. The Book of Genesis opens up with **"In the beginning God created the heavens and the earth."** *Its design was to be paradise for us, starting with Adam and Eve before their fall. When man was cast out of the garden, there was a separation between him* and God. One day Jesus will establish His kingdom again here on earth. The second Heaven would be the angelic realm. That's where angels and demons dwell. The invisible realm is what we cannot see with our human eyes. Remember earlier, when I said that Satan was referred to as, "Prince of the power of the air." The term "air" means that of the invisible world. We can feel the air we breathe, but can't see it. The spirit world acts in that same way.

The third Heaven is a place that is far beyond our comprehension. Some scholars as well as theologians that say there are many dimensions and orders to the Heavens. The Bible we read gets as high as the third. When Jesus shed His blood on the cross, He rose on the third day and was seated at the right hand of the Father. God cannot dwell with sin. That is why he turned his face away from Jesus when he was dying. Remember what Jesus said while dying, **"My God, my God, why have you forsaken me?"** That was because God had to separate Himself until the job was finished. Jesus was bearing all of our sins, and when that very drop of blood was shed and fell to the ground, we would have the opportunity to inherit eternal life.

The devil and his party believed that when Jesus died that was the end of Him. Unfortunately, the devil's plans were ruined. His every attempt throughout Scripture was to make Jesus a victim. That was the worst thing he could do. At first, he made every attempt to stop male children from living after birth. He tried killing the first born when it was said that the Messiah has come. At that point, Satan made all the attempts to see Jesus crucified by working through high authorities in power, the Romans.

Little did he realize that killing Jesus meant eternal life for the sinner. We then were able to receive the free gift of salvation. The ability to enter into the third Heaven can only be accessed through the blood of Christ. When Jesus died, we gained the ability to enter into the throne room of grace. The devil had the position to go back and forth into the presence of God. In Chapter 1 of the Book of Job, it talks about Satan having the ability to be in the presence of the Lord at will. We become higher than the angels, and that's why Satan despises us so much, because we will go where he has been cast out of forever.

The enemy uses so many different tactics to detour our minds that it would take years to figure all of them out. The fall of Adam and Eve were his first two victims. The devil deceived them while in the Garden of Eden. You could say that the devil started building his church using Adam and Eve as his first disciples. The devil used more of a cunning approach (appearing as a serpent). He deceived the woman into believing that her eyes would be opened, and she would be like God. The problem was that she new what God commanded, yet she still bought into the enemy's story. All we need to do is converse with the enemy, and he will twist the truth with a lie. Ignorance is the devil's playground. Of course, she could not be the only one to fall. She convinced Adam to eat of the fruit as well. When being confronted by God, they blamed one another. That is when chaos and sin entered the world. The serpent's trick worked, and they betrayed God. Therefore, the enemy carried out his mission from there until this present day.

The tempter used three resources to entice Eve. We will take it from the Book of 1 John (2:16),

*"**For all that is in the world is lust of the flesh, lust of the eyes, and the pride of life**." The three are what cause us all to sin. The circumstances change for each of us, but the pattern stays the same. The devil uses those three fleshly desires as a guideline for us to fall every time. Eve was enticed by the fruit, because it was pleasant to the eye, tasty to eat, but her pride destroyed her. She was too proud to tell God that she sinned. Eve blamed the devil and Adam blamed Eve. The serpent convinced her she would be equal to God if she ate of the tree. Take a look at the diagram I have made, then we will compare it to today's living. You will notice not much has changed.*

1) Lust of the eyes
(Things we see that look pleasant to the eye.)
2) Lust of the flesh
(Things we feel that satisfy our carnal flesh.)
3) Pride of life
(We want to be better than anyone else.)

These three cover a wide area of sin that is in our lives every day. If one doesn't cause us to fall, there are two more from which the devil may choose. I figured roughly; each category holds about twenty to thirty different ways to fall into sin daily. That is about 60–90 missiles that are launched against us daily. That just covers what we can see with our own eyes. It does not even tap into thoughts daily. Because God knows our own thoughts as well, we can think of a horrible act and be charged as if we performed the physical act itself. I know it sounds crazy, but that is what our enemy uses for ammo against us. When you lust after someone sexually in your own mind, it is just as severe as performing the act itself. Sound weird? I'll explain. The simple fact is this: It was a thought before it ever became reality. Our behavior in life first takes place in our minds because that is how our body functions. The mind tells us what we want then the body responds to what is told. It is up to us whether we entertain a thought or filter it out through our mind. That is why the war we fight is invisible. Let me break it down for you as simply as I can.

The enemy gathers our weaknesses by what he sees. He then goes to work holding what I would like to call cue cards (visual pictures) in front of us, which pollute our thoughts. It is up to us whether we entertain that thought or filter it out. The Bible refers to the enemies' weapons as "darts."

These darts are fired at us every time we are confronted with a specific sin that hinders our walk with the Lord. Try to ponder this thought. Imagine how long a dart is fired at us before it manifests into the natural. It may have been months before we actually acted upon it. The chemical agent could have lived a long time inside of our minds waiting for the right time to strike. The enemy fires away each time he sees a weakness in us. Eventually, our minds become completely corrupted with evil thoughts that we entertain every day of our lives. Since our nature is of a sinful one, we cannot defeat it unless our minds are renewed and transformed into the likeness and image of Christ.

The situations and events that take place in our lives are altered by the words that are spoken. The words we speak are heard by those around us, *but they are also heard by those that are unseen. Our voices carry out into the heavenly realm, and that's how a prayer gets answered. This doesn't mean just praying with an audible voice; God can still hear our inner voice. Our faith in God and our confessions are heard by the words we speak boldly into the atmosphere. God then hears His children, and if it His will, they are manifested into the natural. Then BANG! Your prayer becomes answered. In the (KJV) Book of Hebrews (11:1) it states; "*Now faith is the substance of things hoped for, the evidence of things not seen*." It is our faith that brings it to pass. Everything that God has for us is already there. It's our faith in him that allows us to get what we ask for, within His will. Our faithfulness and obedience pleases God's heart. You need to know that God would never send you anything bad or something that is not of His will, just to make you happy. For example, take someone who is falling short of rent at the end of the month because they have had a slow week at work. That calls for God's help in the matter. Now if you had the money for rent and decided to blow it foolishly by drinking, then chances are God will turn the other way.*

It is important to know that wants and needs work the same way with God as they do with life here on earth. It is time to talk about the other side of the invisible realm. The demons are more than willing to assist you in a specific area of your life that calls for revenge against someone. For example, say someone really is bothering you, and you just want to let him or her have it for whatever reason. It would be your actions and words intensifying, as the little voices signal you to do harm to that person. Let's try this one. You have not touched drugs in years, and you are right where you want to be in God's will. Something happens to put you over the edge, and Satan then fires those cue cards of the good old days when you did drugs. He then entices you with visual images that only make you want to do it even more. Then out of nowhere, friends and people of your past start to come around in perfect timing to cause you to stumble. When all is said and done and you are not strong enough in God, you fall. Physical addiction is a tough thing to break as it is, but when you get help from other parties you cannot see or are not aware of, it can be devastating without God in control. The trick of the enemy is to convince the world that bad things are going to happen to people. That it is just a part of life. Believe this, if you only knew what went on behind the scenes, it would definitely make you second-guess your true purpose and meaning for existing. If you could jump out of your body and see what God sees and knows, you would not be able to beg for forgiveness fast enough.

You need to realize that if you are not on the winning team, you are on the losing side. To sum it all up (you might not like what I have to say), if the Lord is not your Redeemer, then that puts you on Satan's side. I do not mean that you choose to be. The very fact is that whether you are a good person or not, unless you choose Christ as your Savior, the enemy becomes your newfound master. I would never say that if Jesus Himself didn't mention it in Scripture. In the Gospel of John (8:42), Jesus states, **"If God were your father, you would love me, for I proceeded forth and came from God.** *" Jesus then goes on to say in verse 43,* **"Why do you not under-**

stand my speech? Is it because you are not able to understand my speech? *" The punch line is really in verse 44.* **"You are of your father the devil, and the desires of your father you want to do.** *" KJV*

One cannot serve two masters. The devil comes to an individual for three main reasons. That which is to kill, steal, and destroy, as said in the Book of John (10:10). Let's take a look at the three motives our enemy has and see how they can work in our lives.

1) Steal: To rob what God has planned for us, to snatch us away and inherit our souls.
2) Kill: Ourselves and each other.
3) Destroy: The destruction of our lives, friends, jobs, and homes.(All does refer to physical aspects as well as spiritual death.)

Did you ever wonder why we commit the same sins over and over again? Even though we tell ourselves time and time again that we won't commit them, we still do. The Bible refers to them as "demonic strongholds." These occur when the enemy takes our biggest fleshly weaknesses and reminds us of a specific sin in our lives. For example, when first becoming a new Christian, we were plagued with fleshly and carnal weaknesses in our lives. Take someone who had three major sins that he would commit regularly in his life before coming to the Lord. Say there were two areas of sin in his life that he didn't considered as being so bad in his or her mind.

For example:
    1. Alcohol

2. Gambling
3. Adultery
4. Cursing
5. Gossiping

The Christian may have managed to get rid of the first three without a problem, but had two other areas for the enemy to work with. Now cursing and gossiping could turn out to be the main focus of sin. The enemy then takes what you considered to be a moderate problem and brings havoc to your life with what you believed to think as minor. Do not allow the devil to put you in areas where you will be defeated. You may have thought that alcohol, adultery, and gambling were the worst to rid of, but you still left yourself open to defeat. Realize that all areas of sin need to be worked on. You will end up going through life never fully being aware that you need help in a certain area of weakness. We are content dealing with the serious sins, but in fact, all are serious when serving God. We will never be perfect, but the more we ask the Lord to help us deal with our issues, and then we will notice a big change in many ways. It is apparent that we will stumble occasionally, but I guarantee not as frequently, if we follow certain guidelines.

I think one of the toughest realities to face is the fact that the unseen world exists. We are so used to the term "Seeing is believing" that we can't fathom anything else. Unless we can touch it or see it, we do not believe it is real. That is the problem with living in a materialistic world. I could not believe for the longest time that demons were real. In fact, I battled it for quite some time. Because I *wrote stories and watched a lot of horror movies, I was able to replace what I couldn't see with images. I pictured those thoughts until I had enough depth to understand. Then once I knew demons were real, I wished some Hollywood creature were terrifying my only fears. You are probably saying to yourself,* How does he know they are real? Did he ever see one?

I will say this: I have been in the presence of the Lord, when I could not even contain myself from His awesome glory. The warmth and love I had felt were the only reasons for the peace that I felt. I also have sensed the pure presence of evil as well.

It was a cold and blistery night. I was sitting with my daughter's mother in the living room watching television. We were watching Alysha playing on the floor with some toys. My dog was just hanging out, lying next to the sliding glass door. All of a sudden, I sensed an eerie feeling. My skin started to crawl. I was stricken with fear. The chill in the air was too overwhelming for me. I started to shake as if the heat had been off for hours. I tried to downplay it so Heather would not sense that I was scared. The only way I could describe it was by comparing it to being frightened after watching a scary movie; only I was an adult who was just sitting there watching television with the lights on. It was just a few seconds later, when Heather said to me that she felt something strange as well. I knew then it was no coincidence, so we prayed immediately. Within seconds after praying, the presence had left. During that next Bible study, I mentioned to my friend, Chris, what had happened. He said that it was normal when you first become a Christian that the enemy will try to put a "spirit of fear" in a place that worships God.

It was a test of your faith. Sometimes, God will open up your eyes and show you what is around you in the spirit world. God can show us amazing things if we allow him to work in our lives. Just be sure you are ready to know what you are asking to be shown; it can be quite different.

As we wrap up this chapter, I would like to say a few things about warfare. The enemy can hinder our prayer lives with two sins that he thrives on, anger and shame. When we pray to the Lord for a specific need, He answers us, and we feel on top of the world. When we are angry about a certain circumstance, it can be hard to find the strength to pray. It can also be hard to keep praying when the Lord does not answer our prayers, as we would often like Him to. That is when the enemy will try to convince us that maybe we should take the situation into our own hands. Shame is another good path for deception. If we stumble, the enemy will try to make us feel bad for what we have done. He will cause us to feel ashamed and not ask God for forgiveness. Before you know it, weeks can go by before you ever truly repent. Know that God never leaves our sides. Our sins sometimes can block communication with God. When Adam felt he had sinned in the garden, he hid from God. The Lord then went looking for him saying, "Where are you?" The same goes for us today. I know this all seems hard to grasp, especially if you are a skeptic. However, imagine that all I am saying is true (which it is), then what would you have to lose? Our time on earth is but a second in God's eyes. Imagine your number has come up, and what if all you have been taught, yet did not pay attention to, was real? There is no turning back. There is no waking up from a horrible dream. You now find your-self faced with the consequence of decision that you chose. Why? What did it gain for you here on earth? You cannot take anything back with you. Was living a materialistic life in sin worth that much? That, my friends, is the battle we face every day.

I hope this chapter gave you a clearer picture of how warfare really works. Satan is a destroyer with no truth in him. He is a fowler, a wolf, a thief, a serpent, and a dragon. His whole plan and pur-pose is to blind the sight of the world, so that he robs you of all blessings God has in store for you. We will never be perfect and without sin. However, we do not have to be held in chains to our sins either. We can live our lives sinless, to the extent of doing whatever we can possibly do to avoid deliberate sin. However, you cannot allow the enemy to lead you to believe that you are not worthy of having a relationship with God, just because you do fall to sin. The Bible states that God is faithful and just to forgive us of our sins and cleanse us from all unrighteousness.

(4)
A COUNTERFEIT SYSTEM

I am going to keep this chapter short and sweet. I want to give you the heads up on how our enemy is a great impersonator. You need to know that Satan represents everything opposite from where God stands. God is love, while the devil is hate. God brings life, while the enemy destroys it. Of course, a skeptic might say that nature has a way of balancing things and in some cases that is true, but it goes much deeper. If you follow the Scriptures from the beginning until the end, you would find that whatever God did, the devil tried to do even better.

The number seven is God's sign of completion while the number six signifies imperfection. You need to know that the Holy Trinity is made up of the Father, Son, and Holy Spirit. The devil also has his own trinity he goes by. That would be the dragon, beast and, false prophet. God sent His Son to save the world, while the devil will be sending his own (the Antichrist) to destroy it. The Lamb is a representation of Jesus and used for sacrifices in the Old Testament, while the goat is used in certain satanic rituals. It is apparent that the enemy tries to glorify himself as a god. The Bible is full of miracles God had performed, but in reality, the devil will also perform his own miracles. When the Antichrist comes to power, he will appear as an angel of light performing counterfeit miracles. The world will be so amazed that they will think he is the Messiah returning. The beast (Antichrist) will also be able to bring on sickness, as well as take it away. That would be through the power of the dragon (the devil).

The Book of Revelation has the rise and fall of Satan and his forces. Unfortunately, some things must take place before God ultimately destroys the enemy. The Antichrist will appear showing signs and wonders, convincing the world that he is God. The world will marvel at him, and all the people who do not know God's Word will be deceived by his greatness. There will be some of God's people also fooled by the beast when he signs a peace treaty with Israel. You can find that in the Book of Daniel (9:27). The devil's trick will be to make you believe he is, in fact, the returning Christ, but a true believer will know Jesus as He appears out of the sky, when all will see His glory. The Lord will not return as a man, but as a King coming down from Heaven.

It is just a fact of simplicity and reading Scripture that allows you to avoid deception by such false doctrine. Remember, if it does not line up with the Word of God, it is a lie of the devil. There will be some people unaware of the Antichrist, but other people will be giving the devil his due as well. It states in 2 Corinthians 11:13, **"For such are false apostles, deceitful workers of the devil transforming themselves into apostles of Christ."** *KJV*

I hope you realize the importance and understanding that there is a system that counterfeits God's intentions. Do not fall to the bait of Satan, but rather look unto God's Word. I thank God for the Holy Spirit, who can lead us into all truth. We will talk about the Spirit of God in another chapter, but for now, know that He seals the saved and regenerates the sinner. That, my friend, is the main reason for trusting in God's Word. I believe at one time or another we all have had someone we wanted to be like. If we did not look up to them in a positive manner, we would look upon them with a form of envy. The enemy is just that, envious and jealous. The devil, though he tries, cannot give you eternal life and take the credit for creating a human race such as ours. In the end, they too will be judged as well and cast into the lake of fire, along with everyone else who did not receive salvation. You need to know that hell was created for Satan and his angels alone. It will be man who decides his own final destination. Unfortunately, many will perish, but it will not be by God's choice. That is why we all need to realize the warfare we are up against and know how it can alter our eternity.

Darkness may copy light to a certain extent, but as we talked about at the beginning of this book, they cannot dwell together. A lit area always wipes out the darkness. There will even be a time when the darkness will not exist at all. Until then, know there is a counterfeit system that will strive to be better than God. They will do whatever it takes to sway souls into thinking this is all a lie. Man lives his life by following a certain pattern. He works hard, raises children, and enjoys taking vacations. There are also the single-type people. They will buy all sorts of toys for themselves and go to fancy restaurants. They also enjoy sports and going to strip clubs with their friends. No matter how you break it down, we are caught in a ticking trap waiting for our number to come up. There must be a thought in your mind that asks, Is this it? Is this all that life has to offer?

The truth is that we're living in the counterfeit system, and it is not of God. He never intended for us to struggle with the everyday grind. When man fell to sin, he was on his own, doing it his way and look where it got him. He made the enemy his god.

After man was kicked out of the Garden, he made up his own laws and followed a system that was imperfect. While God wanted restoration, man was too busy worshiping the creature rather than the Creator. The enemy has programmed man to rely on his emotions, such as anger, envy, and deceit.

*We are so occupied worshiping other gods that we forget a lot of things we once were brought up to believe. There are three things in life that cause man to kill. They are greed, lust, and anger. You need to understand that the world and everything in it comprise a purely an evil environment, built entirely upon profit. So the answer is very simple. The counterfeit system is the world that we live in right now. I can say that, standing firm on Scripture, because it states in the Book of James (4:4). "***Whosoever therefore will be a friend of the world, is an enemy of God.***" It is important to realize that we are in this world, but are not of this world. Jesus says in the Gospel of John (15:19), "***If you were of this world, the world would love his own: but because you are not of this world, but I have chosen you out of this world, therefore the world hates you.***"*

I close this chapter with a final thought. There are two masters and each has his own laws. It would be safe to say that most of us would choose a favorable side. The scary part is that there are people who will actually serve God Sunday through Thursday, but look to the devil come Friday and Saturday eve-

nings by going out to clubs. These are the ones who need to make a choice; we can't play each side for gain. God knows whose side you are really on, and in the end, God will judge each and every one of us.

Over the next few chapters, we are going to take a look at how the enemy operates in our daily lives. The things we do in our recreational time can change the outcome. I like to call it "secret doom." It's when we are unaware that we are being attacked. We will view certain topics, and then I will give you some fundamental skills in fighting the opposition.

(5)
SATAN VS. MUSIC

This is indeed the toughest topic I could discuss. I had struggled with it for years, especially because I played drums and was a big part of the music trend. It is safe to say that music is just as potent as any drug we could feed ourselves. It is inspirational. It can release aggression and also stimulate sexuality. It is no wonder Satan seeps through each note, dominating the airwaves with his perversion. Remember that he was in charge of music at one time. He can surely stir up a beat here on earth.

If we sit and listen to praise and worship music, we can feel, in our spirit, a very warm and positive feeling that touches our hearts and is very uplifting. Now listening to music on a non-spiritual level, we would be able to feel an adrenalin rush that goes right through us. We listen to music when we are happy, sad, in love, or sometimes to just sit back and reflect on past memories of our lives. If we are angry, we tend to become violent with certain songs we hear. Let us now look at the few topics that music possesses and offers its listeners.

1. Happiness
2. Sadness
3. Love
4. Anger

By looking at those four categories, it is safe to say that if the devil were to attack us, it would be through emotions, our emotions. That is why music plays a big part in his overall plan. It affects people of all ages. It does not matter what style of music it is either. There is a lot of wonderful music in every category that will suit all of our needs. This is where is gets very complex and deceiving, so please pay attention carefully. You can think you have filtered out negative music by changing a certain style, but in all actuality, you have allowed the enemy to come at you with a new sound that's more pleasing to your ears. The same deception can be used against you. Take someone who listens to hard-core rock music that is very negative. Say he ends up switching to a much more soothing and relaxing sound to relieve his ears. The music might have changed, but the lyrics may have remained. See, a loud guitar to a soft piano only became light in sound. In reality, the subliminal messages became softer as well. It becomes harder to hear what the song is actually trying to say.

I can sit here and scream as loudly as I can about how I hate someone. I can also speak softly about how someone has hurt me, and I still cannot seem to find it in my heart to forgive him or her. You would tend to think the second statement that I said was understanding. In reality, I am still talking about unforgiveness. See, it is how we react to something that is said, but the meaning is the same. We listen to the soft-spoken voice, and it becomes deceiving to us. We tend to become deaf and block it out. We can even say, "But I only like that song for the music not the lyrics." It is still corrupting us, because the words are entering our subconscious minds, whether we know it or not. Sometimes the music can be just as corrupting without the lyrics.

Picture yourself at a club dancing. The colored lights and fog machine have entered the dance floor. The music is loud and jamming. You can feel the bass drum piercing through your body, and everyone is dancing and feeling the music. It is apparent during the course of the night that lust will enter the minds of those around you. If some do not engage in fleshly acts with a partner, surely the thought is there, whether it is for just a split second or all night. That is how the enemy operates in music. He uses the more-talented entertainers as his vessels, without them even knowing it. The enemy will also help with thoughts to a writer whose voice will be heard all over the world, making sure he becomes rich and full of pride or until his message is heard. That is the anointing that the devil possesses in music. There are many gifted musicians out there with positive, great music. The problem is, unless the music is about the Lord and his salvation, it's just noise to God's ears. God has given everyone a special talent, but unfortunately, He can't bless us unless we are glorifying him. Today's music talks about death, killing, revenge, love, or sex. God wants forgiveness and salvation that lets the whole world know that Jesus Christ is Lord.

Music today signifies sexuality. With movies and books, they all serve the same purpose. It really gets complex with warfare and music. A musician who is talented, but operates under a worldly realm, is a target in sending mixed messages to the world. The problem is that when you are operating outside of the anointing of the Holy Spirit, the devil can assist you *with his own. I don't mean that we can't write about everyday life with all the intentions of meaning it for good. Sometimes we don't even have to write lyrics to send a negative message. The instrumental part of music can affect our thoughts. That is why we can listen to a soundtrack score from a movie and feel an eerie chill. What is the first thing that comes to mind when we think of a certain movie that may have scared us? It is the music.* **"Away with the noise of your songs! I will not listen to the music of your harps. But let justice roll on like a river."** *Amos 5:25*

I suggest that you seek the Lord when it comes to this matter. Try a new approach that soothes your mind with music pleasing to the Lord. Cleanse your mind with a pure heart that will enable you to draw near to God. There is a variety of Christian music for you to listen to. There is Christian rap, as well as rock for the listener who likes a heavier sound. God bless you all as you receive wisdom in this matter.

(6)
EVIL SPIRITS

We are now going to take a look at the power source behind our weaknesses. We will discuss the demonic realm of fallen angels known as demons, the reapers that sow despair for all of us who are Christians as well as nonbelievers. Some may get confused thinking demons only affect the believer, because they have created visions in their minds that only religious people believe in them. To a nonbeliever, the Bible is nothing more than a brainwashing method to generate money. The funny thing is that warfare will work against the nonbeliever better than the believer will.

A demon's job is very simple. It is to keep you in doubt whether you believe or not. Each evil spirit is assigned to different tasks in our lives. Remember, a third fell from Heaven. That does not necessarily mean a small amount either, compared to the number of angels in Heaven. If I were to guess, I would probably say millions fell. A demon will attack each one of us according to our lifestyles. They see from above and view how we operate. Then they take instructions from their commander and chief and set forth to destroy us.

These reapers will discourage the believer into thinking he cannot prosper any further. Once we are sealed with the Holy Spirit, we are new targets to be assassinated. They recognize who we are, and believe it or not, they know us all by name. A demon will see to it that an unbeliever stays blinded to the truth. The job becomes much easier as the person gets deeper in the realm of sin. The demons will move on to someone else, but always keeping tabs on their former clients. The only way he knows where to go is to look for whose light is on in the bedroom. Picture in your mind a spirit hovering around the earth in the Heavens, seeing nothing but total darkness. As long as there is no light shining, the demon has his district in order. As soon as some light pops up, it calls for immediate attention. The spirit then reports to a higher officer and finds out more information about the light that is cluttering its zone.

Spirit's have names. The Bible is full of the evil spirits that Jesus dealt with. It would be only right that they knew our names as well. In the Book of Acts, the Jewish priests tried to cast out devils by their own authority without knowing Jesus. The Jewish exorcist then said to the evil spirit, "I cast you out in the name of Jesus whom Paul preaches." The first mistake was that they did not have Jesus from within. They only followed what they heard Paul preach.

The evil spirit then turned to the man and said, "Jesus I know, Paul I know, but who are you?" The second mistake was trying to do battle with satanic forces, with no authority in Heaven. The result was that the men received the beating of their lives. It was so bad that they fled out of the house naked and wounded. Without Jesus, you cannot defeat a demon. They are excessively powerful for a man to defeat. Today, in warfare, it works the same. The evil spirits know who we are as believers.

Demons are not omnipresent. They cannot be everywhere at once. Like the devil, they can only act by what they see or by our behavior dealing with fleshly desires. We are now going to look at a chart I made and expose the different evil spirits that deal in all facets of sin. All were taken from the Bible. You need to be aware of spiritual deception on all levels.

1. Spirit of divination (Acts 16:16)
2. Familiar spirits (Deuteronomy 18:11)
3. Lying spirits (2 Chronicles 18:22)
4. Perverse spirits (Isaiah 19:14)
5. Spirit of haughtiness (Proverbs 16:18)
6. Spirit of heaviness (Isaiah 61:3)
7. Spirit of infirmity (Luke 13:11)
8. Deaf and dumb spirit (Mark 7:32)
9. Spirit of bondage (Romans 8:15)
10. Legion (Mark 5:9)
11. Spirit of fear (2 Timothy 1:7)
12. Seducing spirits (1Timothy 4:1)
13. Spirit of Antichrist (1 John 4:3)
14. Spirit of error (1 John 4:6)

These spirits are those our fleshly desires deal with every day. It is important for you to know that they have names according to our weaknesses. When sin entered into man back in the garden, we were cursed with sinful afflictions as we were separated from God. The Lord never intended for us to die or get sick. We were cursed by man's choice, not God's. Even if a demon did not cause a specific disease, our infirmities are still a result of the curse.

For instance, when we lie, it does not always mean that a demon made us do it, but lying is a sin.

A demon could take that sin and be that inner voice that tells us to do it more and more. Because lying is a weakness one may have, the evil spirit just intensifies the sensation for sin. Let us take "fear" as a topic. A spirit who knows someone is fearful will think of ways to make him even more afraid. It preys on weakness. Now giving into that fear, which is sin according to the Bible, only puts us in a trapped state of mind. God did not give us a spirit of fear, as Timothy said. Let us look at some demonic merits that branch off from fear, and you decide if you think God wants you to feel this way.

1. Nightmares
2. Anxiety
3. Phobia

All can make us paranoid, which can result to continuous torment in our minds. Now look at what it can do to us spiritually, if we do not believe God can help us deal with our fears. We tend to lose our faith, which is exactly what the demon wants. Once the demon knows we have no faith in a matter, he will try and finish us off. The result of fear is that it strikes us hard. We can work ourselves right into a heart attack. Remember what the Book of James says. **"When sin is conceived, it brings forth death."**

Satan and his forces are not just content with tormenting us as believers, but their whole plan is to see us die. The fewer believers that are in the world, the more power the enemy can gain through God's army decreasing. It is important that we be able to sort out the differences between demonic activity and emotional, psychological, and physical problems. Someone who is angry will most likely vent his or her anger in some sort of way. A violent outburst is a humanistic, emotional response due to a situation. The reason for that act is due to the impulses of fallen human nature. Let's take it one step further. A person who has really big, violent outbursts with superhuman strength could, in fact, have what we call "demon-oppression."

There are two types of demonic activity in a person. That would be oppression and possession.

1) Oppression: One who is demonically influenced by spiritual forces surrounding the individual, causing him or her to behave a certain way they are not usually known for doing.

2) Possession: Demonic spiritual forces invade one's body physically.

Let's look at the signs and attributes of demonic possession. It can include the following:

1. Change in physical strength
2. Change in voice
3. Seizures or foaming at the mouth
4. Schizophrenia
5. Speaking in different tongues
(language unknown, sometimes Latin)

Once again, you need to make sure that the signs are genuine. There are mental and physical defects that can cause actual medical problems. Meaning, not everyone who has seizures is possessed. However, you need to know that physical and mental imperfections are the result of the curse. Before we were separated from God, we were in fact made perfect in His likeness and image. There were no imperfections and impurities.

Mark 5:1–9 talks about Legion, a spirit who had many unnatural powers. The Book of Luke (9:39) talks about one who had convulsions. Demons also have knowledge of things largely hidden to human beings, a pre-knowledge. So if one does not know the Lord and is dabbling in a form of witchcraft, he or she may actually believe he or she has the ability to see into the future. I feel that many people who deal with the occult are actually receiving information from a demonic spirit.

Demons will mix lies with the truth. They can take their knowledge of what they know, and then they convince people with enough evidence to make them believe a specific lie. They are masters in this field. So where do these demons hang out when they are not possessing or oppressing someone? These pests find homes where sin is welcomed with open arms. They will dwell in nightclubs, where adultery and fornication are taking place. The next place would be an exotic entertainment establishment, where certain acts of perversion can transpire. The tricky part is, they don't need to be in a titled facility to dwell. They don't necessarily need an invitation either. They are content with dwelling in some local church or even our very own homes.

Remember, God does not dwell in temples made with hands, as said in Acts 7:48. Our temple is within us. Therefore, we must make sure our hearts and spirits are right before God. If a church is made up of believers who are not in line with Scripture and the Holy Spirit is not active, then chances are, demons will hang around looking for new Christian spirits to lead astray. That is how there were so many religions discovered, by corrupt spirits blinding people with false doctrine. As far as our homes, well, it works the same way. If we do not make sure our household is in line with God's order, we can allow certain activities and people to enter our houses, attached with some demonic influence.

The Book of Genesis says in 4:7, "**Sin lies at the door, and its desire is for you.**" Jesus also said in Matthew 12:43–45, "**When an unclean spirit goes out of a man he goes through dry places, seeking rest, and finds none. Then he says I will return to the house from which I came. And when he comes, he finds it empty, swept, and put in order. Then he goes and takes with him seven other spirits more wicked than himself, and they enter and dwell there; and the last state of a man is much worse then the first. So shall it also be with this wicked generation.**"

Let's take a look at this passage. It says that an evil spirit goes through dry places to find rest. The term "dry places" in the literal sense means hot arid places where no water or life can survive. In a spiritual sense, it can mean the same thing—places where the Holy Spirit does not dwell or live—a church, a house, or any place where there is no spiritual life. Another key factor—if your house is not kept in order, whether it be within you or a location, then a particular spirit will come back with more help, far more wicked than itself.

Jesus cast out many devils in the New Testament. Luke 10:19 says we are to cast out devils, because Jesus gave us all the power and authority over the enemy. Some demons cannot be cast out by command either. When the apostles had trouble casting out an evil spirit, Jesus said this particular one can only come out by prayer and fasting. In warfare, it can become very tricky. In the Book of Daniel (10: 12–13), Daniel's prayers were heard as soon as he prayed to God, but due to warfare, the enemy withstood the angel and Daniel's prayer was hindered for twenty-one days.

Demons are so good at confusion and chaos that when you are aware of their tricks, it's a charge to see them exposed and ignored. Things start to happen when your spiritual eyes are opened, and you're well grounded in the Lord. Sometimes a situation becomes serious involving demonic activity, while some smaller things become hilarious when you are well aware of their little stunts. It was funny to see it every time we prepared to pray on Tuesday night Bible studies. The phone would ring like clockwork. It was always around 7:30 p.m. or so. You can bet any other night that it never rang at that time. Once we ignored and exposed the spirit, the phone never rang again. Another time at Bible study, during prayer, the door opened wide and slammed shut. Everyone at the study felt a sense of evil begin to fill the room. I'll tell you this last one then we will move on. I had finished breaking away from someone who claimed she loved me. I do believe that she cared for me, but adultery was not on my "To Do" list. The funny part was that I felt that if I did not break away, sin would haunt my flesh until I fell victim to desires of the flesh. I felt I had passed a certain test God was giving me. The funny thing was, shortly after that, a woman whom I had not spoken to in years called me out of nowhere, wanting to take me out drinking. The enemy works in the most subtle ways if we do not catch him.

There is so much to learn about demons. Know the basic tricks and get a firm idea of whom you are dealing with. We will talk about how to defeat these fowl spirits in another chapter, but for now, here are a few ideas to help discipline your spiritual walk as a Christian.

1. Choose friends wisely. (Make sure they are Spirit-filled believers.)
2. Stay away from temptations that bind you with specific sins (addictions that you overcame).
3. Stay away from places that lust and perversions dominate. (Once you are in Satan's lair, it's hopeless.)
4. Always pray. The Holy Spirit will guide you into discernment concerning any demonic activity.

There is so much that I could tell you about fallen angels. It would be too complex for you to contain all of it. The dark side is such of an elite force that if Jesus is not in your life, you are surely doomed to destruction, whether you believe or not. Some of these angels were so vicious back in the days of Noah that they were cast in prison before their time. In Genesis 6:6, it talks about the sons of God taking women unto themselves, causing a race of giants. Some scholars believe that when they talk about the "Sons of God" they are referring to angelic beings. If you read, further in 1 Peter 3:19–20, it says "**Jesus went and preached to the spirits in prison, who formerly were disobedient when once the divine**

longsuffering waited in the days of Noah. *" If that is true, then they must have been such a dangerous threat to the earth and man that God had them thrown in everlasting chains far before their time.*

We can learn so much if we study the Scriptures. Some scholars believe that the "Sons of God" were in fact a wicked race of angels who existed before the flood. It is said that the angels, who were cast out of Heaven, actually took women unto themselves. They were said to have created a race of giants, half man and half demon called "Nephilim." God, being furious with man and creation, saw how wicked the world had become and caused a great flood throughout the world that wiped out humankind. Coincidently, Goliath, who David fought, was a giant. These angels held high ranks in Heaven before their fall to earth. Even in the angelic realm, there was an order to be followed. It's not to say that all this is true biblical fact, but it was said that the prophet, Enoch, was shown these visions by certain angels of rank—that he was the only one to come face-to-face with God Himself. Unfortunately, we can't hold that as anything concrete.

I do not want to overemphasize the study of the demonic realm as being all-powerful. God is all the power we need to defeat Satan, but until you hit that level of authority, you need to be geared up and ready. There is a spirit in this world that is very dangerous to man. Man can go either way at anytime. A man cannot serve two masters. Remember that they will love one and hate the other.

I leave you with one thought as we conclude this chapter. We read earlier in this book that if we "Resist the devil; he will flee." When Jesus was in the desert, the tempter used different tactics to try and sway our Lord in failing. Look at the way each passage in Mathew 4 was directed.

"The devil came . . ." Matt 4: 3
"The devil took . . ." Matt 4: 5
"The devil showed . . ." Matt 4: 8
"The devil left . . ." Matt 4: 11

Jesus resisted the devil three times by using Scripture to defeat him. When we feel the enemy trying to tempt us, we are to use the same authority as Jesus did. When the devil comes and takes us to a place and shows us a temptation, we are to resist it. It's when we act on it that we fall, just like Eve. She was tempted by what she saw. You also need to know this final thought about demonic forces. It is very important to know that a demon, or someone influenced by one, can still say that they believe in the Lord. That is how warfare can become so tricky. The fact is that if you take away one part of the Trinity, then you are truly not a believer. You cannot have God the Father, God the Son, without God the Holy Spirit. Nor can you believe in God, but not Jesus.

"Not everyone who says to me," Lord, **Lord will enter the kingdom of heaven.**"

-Matthew 7: 21

(7)
SPIRITUAL ARMOR

We have just talked about how demonic forces work in our lives. We also discussed the battle in the Heavens between good and evil. You may be wondering if there is anything you can do to fight against a demonic attack? The answer is yes. It is time to share with you the advantage of being on the winning team. To become a spirit warrior for God's ultimate force, you must have your spiritual armor.

For any athlete to play a sport, he or she must be equipped with the right gear to wear in order to perform to his or her fullest. A boxer cannot enter a ring without gloves and a mouthpiece. A football player can't enter the gridiron without a helmet and protective padding. A spirit warrior cannot enter the big, heavenly arena without his or her gear as well. The Bible explains in Ephesians, Chapter 6, that we are to put on the full armor of God. Of course, our armor is invisible to the eye, but if you remember, we had established earlier in this book that our struggles are not against flesh and blood. The Bible compares our gear to a Roman soldier doing battle. We will look at the passage, and then I will break it down for you to get an idea of its true meaning. Let us read from the Book of Ephesians (6:14).

"Stand therefore, having girded your waist with truth, having put on the breastplate of righteousness, having shod your feet with the prep-

aration of the gospel of peace; above all, taking the shield of faith with which you will be able to quench all the fiery darts of the wicked one. And take the helmet of salvation, and the sword of the Spirit, which is the word of God.*"*

Now take this passage and pick out the armor we need for protection. Then look at the meaning in a spiritual sense.

1. Waist
2. Breastplate
3. Feet
4. Shield
5. Helmet
6. Sword

These six items are the gear we need to have in order to face our enemy in the spirit world. We use these devices, not in a literal sense, but a heavenly sense. Let's break down their true meaning and attempt to do what I call "Scripture breakdown." I will try to make sense of it all in the simplest way I know how. Take the opening passage in verse one. "Stand therefore having girded your waist with truth . . ." First, we need to stand firm. A soldier or a fighter needs to have a strong battle stance. Second, we need to have our belt on our waist. That refers to the Word of God. See, it's simple. Part of our gear is standing firm on the Word of God.

The next phrase used is " . . . having put on the breastplate of righteousness." It means that if we are to battle, our chest must be protected. It also means that our hearts must be pure and protected at all times from having an evil heart that is stone cold. We can't allow ourselves to follow something or someone with a heart that devises evil. Let's look at the next verse—"having shod your feet with the preparation of the gospel of peace above all." This term is used to describe a Christian having the ability to walk in light, instead of darkness. He or she must be able to go out and preach the gospel of peace. If someone walks firmly, it usually means that they are confident, but aware of their surroundings with no sign of fear, opposed to one who stomps around uptight and aggressively. They're usually on their guard and ready to snap at the drop of a dime. It may also show insecurity that sends out vibes like, Don't mess with me, I'm not in the mood. Remember, Jesus said, "You will know them by their fruits." He meant our actions, verbally and physically.

The next passage is "taking the shield of faith, which you will be able to quench all the fiery darts of the wicked one." To dodge and protect you from swords and knives, one needs a shield. The term "shield" refers to faith. That protects us from the enemy, who is throwing darts our way. Remember earlier in the book, when I explained darts as our temptations or cue cards, which the enemy may hold up to us randomly? It is our faith that protects us from Satan's scheme to detour our walk with the Lord. We are to fight the enemy by our faith and belief in the Lord.

The last verse is "take the helmet of salvation and the sword of the Spirit, which is the word of God." You would need your head protected from objects that can strike it and cause injury. In a spiritual battle, you need to know your mind and control your thoughts by not allowing Satan to get into your head. As I said before, sin that is conceived first begins with a thought. Your mind is the battlefield. Of course, you not only need defense, but you also need an offense, a weapon to use. That would be your sword. It actually means your Bible, the Word of God. It strikes every time you speak Scripture. That is how we defeat the enemy. Jesus destroyed him with Scripture when He was tempted in the desert by the devil. We can do the same when we face a tempta-tion. It's our defense mechanism in piercing the dark forces and striking them down at any time. When all is said and done, the armor we use is not physical or materialistic. Our spirit is in line with God through the power of the Holy Spirit. Standing firm on God's Word with every step of faith and belief will get us by in this flesh-dominated world. That is the armor that gets us by with another victory point over demonic forces.

The next phase is to prepare us with our armor each day. I like to do a weapons check each morning I wake up. It is good to end in prayer by ask-ing the Lord to make sure all your gear is fully secure before you start your day. Believe me, the devil will not be shy in being the first one to take a shot at you. I remember going out one morning thinking my armor was in complete check. I felt that I was fully ready to start my day. About twenty minutes later, I received a call on my cell phone from a former girlfriend I dated awhile back. Immediately I felt thoughts of lust fill my mind. I was caught up in the moment that I lost track of time. After an hour went by of reminiscing the good old days, we had hung up with one another. Not more than a minute later, it hit me hard. I played into the enemy by not making sure my helmet was in check. I allowed him to challenge me and win without ever fighting back. It was almost as if I could hear him say, "You just prayed, and I got you to have lustful thoughts anyway. You lose." You see, that is how the enemy operates. I also feel that, on occasion, God will test us by allowing circumstances to arise. The funny thing was, I prayed shortly after the incident and never heard from that person again.

The act of warfare is found in the battles that we face, but also in how they arise. We become more in tune to the unseen world as we grow spiritually and realize that these attacks are preplanned to test us each time. The power isn't just the temptation; it's how accurate the timing will occur. For instance, writing this chapter was hard. After I explained the incident about the old girlfriend calling, I received a call while writing this section from a woman that I know. Not only was I distracted, but also my computer shut down, and I had to rewrite the last two pages all over again. The woman was someone I had been friends with for a while. She was telling me how she was unhappy with her marriage and was looking to me for comfort. Not only did I lose the two pages, but I also stopped writing until the next day. It's the timing of it all that proves true warfare, and if you can recognize it, then you will know that you're in the trenches of a messy battle. When you are moving in God's direction, the way He wants you to, the dark forces will try to invade your territory. I'm trying not to get really complicated with this chapter. I just want you to understand this in the simplest way I know how. Someone who does not believe in warfare, or for that matter who isn't a believer in God or the Lord Jesus, will laugh it off as a big joke say-

ing that it's all in your mind. Another good way to describe unbelievers is that they feel life works by the luck of the draw, or something is coincidental. The truth is that they are just pawns falling victim to warfare's ultimate plan. The humanistic way of thinking is "Something we can't see cannot be in control of our destiny." The fact is simple. If you cannot accept spiritual reality in this life, you will on the other side, but it will be too late. We will talk more in another chapter about religion and different beliefs dealing with life after death, but for now, we need to stick with this topic. I agree with one thing; we have not been physically dead to know what's on the other side. I hope that we will be around a lot longer before that time comes (God willing), but we need to really think about the consequences. We can make choices now, but in the life to come, we can't. We already made them when we were alive.

The art of war is simple. Be alert and ready to take a hit, but make sure you're strong enough to get back up and fight. God does not expect us to never fall or fail; He simply wants us to get up knowing what we did and go forward without guilt. As long as we repent and ask for forgiveness, He will meet us halfway. In my case, as I said before, my temptations were women. Therefore, it was no wonder that every time I felt strong the enemy would resurrect some former girlfriend of the past with precise timing. There is so much that could be said about warfare; it would take forever. I am more apt to share with you a little of everything, so that you may become more grounded.

Let us end with a simple guideline on spiritual armor. Pray every morning that God blesses your thoughts, heart, and tongue. Always be aware of your surroundings, physically and spiritually. Know that you're never left unprotected and realize that you're never alone either. Meaning, as much as God is in your life holding your hand, Satan is in the midst of all and every type of chaos in your daily travels. The forces of darkness cannot touch you unless you allow them to by giving into temptations. Even if you overcome one attack, demons are lining up for another to throw at you. Sometimes your mind can get so cluttered with so many thoughts about the spirit world that from time to time you will have wished you were never involved. Don't be disappointed. God has great things in store for those that obey him and keep his commandments. May the Lord bless you in this topic so that you will become a true "Spirit Warrior" and overcome any demonic attack that you may encounter? Remember, our God is greater than any other god in this world. With the power of the blood of Jesus, we will not be moved.

"Put on the full armor of God, so that you will be able to stand firmly against the schemes of the devil. *"* -*Ephesians 6:11*

(8)
SATAN VS. THE NEW AGE

This next topic may be one of the most controversial of all in today's world. It deals with a new lifestyle that will fit our modern way of thinking. There are so many names for this type of practice. Some will say paganism or the occult. Others will identify themselves as being some spiritus, or one who has found balance in nature's forces. One may have a god that he worships or may simply use the term "Higher Power" as his source. The New Age simply puts no boundaries on whom or what it bows down to. "You can create anything as your god, as long as it works for you." Sound familiar?

Some practices involve the worship of nature. The earth, air, water, or fire, you will hear many different ways in developing spirituality. Some will even contact the dead or a loved one for an answer. They claim to channel positive energy while taking negative energy out of your body through a crystal. These are all aspects of the New Age movement. Let us take witchcraft for instance—a popular practice that has existed for hundreds of years. It enables you to cast spells on people or heal the sick with herbs and potions. It makes the occult appear to us as wondrous and free from an eternity of hell. It allows lust to be glorified as love or homosexuality to be acceptable. Think about this for a second, and then ask yourself the question, "Do you think its okay to make love to the same sex?" We would not accept having a relationship with a relative or an animal. We don't think it's okay to rape a child. In fact, we would not agree with any of those things, but homosexuality. . . . We welcome it. Why do you think that is? I'll let you ponder the thought, and by the end of this chapter, give yourself an answer.

God wants us to love and be happy. He also wants us to be healed and live a life of peacefulness. He doesn't ask that we hurt anyone, steal, or murder. There isn't anything out of the ordinary that is required to serve Him. He wants us to remember what his Son did for us and receive the gift of eternal life. There are no rituals to perform, no candles or incense to heal, and no blood sacrifices to increase power. There are no spells to cast for gain or revenge. He simply wants us to trust in Him and to be our Provider, our Avenger, and our Healer.

So why do we refuse those things from Him, but accept them from another source? I can tell you the first reason—deception. The second one—rebellion. People think that as a Christian one can't sin, because when they do, they have already broken the vow of holiness. The truth is that they feel it is impossible to follow such rules, so they find another way to believe in something—something that isn't so complicated to follow. The enemy will fill your head with thoughts that make it impossible to be worthy to serve God. He will tell you that there are other ways to turn, within spirituality, without feeling guilty. As time goes on, your faith in God falls short, and you become rebellious. Thoughts fill your head with thoughts like, I can sin without feeling guilty. This religion understands what I've been seeking to find.

In the end, the devil just wanted you to find another resource other than God himself, something that will accept you for who you are and what you stand for. Worshiping the God of the Bible may appear too complicated for a person to follow because it forces us to be pure and obey the rules of the Creator. All along, evil is glorifying itself as more suitable to our needs. It will use beauty, magic, and sexuality without limit. Evil takes the misfits and gives them hope, believing in something that allows them to fit in. Evil has no rules. Do you think the devil cares what or whom you worship? No, he does not. All he cares about is that you are disobeying God. He is smart enough to know that as long as he keeps your eyes off the truth, then the truth will never set you free. So if it's sex, spells, homosexuality, nature, crystals, Ouija boards, witchcraft, fleshly desires, and fantasy that keep you away, so be it. He even has people who don't believe in anything—no religion—no God under his or her wing. If your belief in miracles is referred to as luck, then he is happy.

We have a God and a devil. We have good and bad. We have positive and negative. We have forgiveness and unforgiveness. We have light and darkness, day and night. There is nothing in between. You are one or the other. The enemy will create a medium if that is what it takes to blind you. It contradicts itself more than you realize. The enemy will have you running in circles for the rest of your life. He will have you trying anything, just to snatch you away from the truth. He will also be the first to throw something in your face that you're doing wrong if you are a Christian. "See, where is your God is now? If you truly worship God, then why are you still sinning?"

He is the "Father of Lies" as we talked about earlier. He is the "Accuser." How could anything he says stand true, when there is no truth in him? A nonbeliever and a Christian have one thing in common, we both sin. The difference is, we can truly ask for repentance and forgiveness. God will see our sincerity and honor that as holy and justifiable. Our flesh will always sin until the day we die, but our spirit will always stand righteous in the eyes of God, if we are His children.

I'm not here to judge what someone is doing or to point the finger at a specific religion or practice. I'm simply here to say that I believe in Scripture, and if my God says that seeking other gods and practices are sin and abominations in his sight, I have to accept it. It was not easy for me. I sought other gods before, and I practiced certain religions. I engaged in witchcraft, actually straight-out Satanism, to seek power and life. I can say that, after all I have been through, I wish I knew the Lord Jesus a long time ago. Before I lowered myself in humility, because I thought what I was doing was right. I am here to say that I was wrong. We need to take more initiative with our children, not letting them feel ashamed to talk to us. We cannot let our children be subjected to a New Age lifestyle, or they will surely suffer in the end. It would be by our own ignorance if they did. God despises many things, but also honors many. Do you think for a second that He is not upset when He sees homosexual marriages being preformed or priests who molest and rape children in a place we call church? I have one thing to say to the nonbeliever out there. First, I pray that you find the Lord. You will need to explain yourself and prepare to be judged for the choices you *have made when He comes back.*

I have no doubt in my mind that some people who engage in these practices are good people. I am sure they are, and their intentions are more positive than negative. The problem is that they were misinformed and misguided by someone or something that affected them as a youth. I cannot help but wonder about those who have never turned away from their practices and have passed away. I am sure that they expected something different on the other side. I wonder how many of them wish they could come back and warn their friends and loved ones who are still here on earth. I hope you all attempt to seek the truth one day, before it is too late.

"When you enter the land that the Lord your God has giving you, do not imitate the detestable customs of those nations. No one among you is to make his son or daughter pass through fire, practice divination, tell fortunes, interpret omens, practice sorcery, cast spells, consult a medium or a familiar spirit, inquire of the dead." - *Deuteronomy 18:9–11*

"If a man sleeps with a man as with a woman, they have both committed an abomination. They must be put to death; their blood is on their own hands." -*Leviticus 20:13*

I feel that we can really touch ground on religion and tie it in with the New Age, all in one chapter instead of separating them individually. The definition of these two topics can be summed up very easily—to put your faith or belief in a certain practice other than what God has said in His word. People tend to take certain things out of the Bible and keep some to fit their way of thinking and living. It works kind of like a new chapter that God never agreed to. Because we're in the "New Age" and times have changed, it's supposedly okay now.

I have heard people say countless times to me, "Well, how do you know that's God's Word? Since man wrote it, he may have made up his own story."

For the longest time I would simply answer them back saying ,"Well, how do you know He didn't?" That always left an unsolved answer to a confusing question.

The fact of the matter is simple. If God is who He said that He is and He is all powerful and all knowing, then why couldn't He see to it that His word got to the people of the world with no tampering? God can raise the dead, heal the sick, and part the Red sea then why couldn't He work and speak through prophets to make sure His word went untouched? When you start to put God in a box, then He has no room to set you free and help you. However, when some crisis arises or a death takes place, what is the first thing you say as a believer or nonbeliever? What is the first thing that comes to mind? "God why?" Well, if you never believed in Him to help you or believed His word fully then why should He answer you? For that matter, why should He listen to you or help you? God is not some cosmic Santa running around in the universe, begging to give you things because He is all alone. It takes faith in God, seeking His Word, and receiving the gift of salvation through Christ Jesus. The devil has no rules except for you to have no commitment to God. I am going to say some things, some basic things that some of you may not have thought about or known for that matter and show you how easy it is to distort God's Word.

First, let's take church for instance. People think that going to church is good enough every Sunday morning. They end up feeling good that they served God forty-five minutes a week and they sin the other six days. If you only put a little time into some-thing, you will only get a little back. A football player who wants to make the NFL one day will not practice only forty-five minutes a week, will he? Second, some churches have been perverted with priests abusing people who confided in them. In certain states, it is now legal to marry a gay couple. How could we then expect to confess our sins to them, when they them-selves are corrupting God's children?.

Let's break those views down. If we know the word, we will understand that when Jesus died on the cross and rose, He became our High Priest. Therefore, we would pray to Him for forgiveness, not man. Why? It's because man is not above the Lord. Jesus' blood gave us access into the throne room of grace. We can enter the Holiest of Holies and com-mune with God because of the gift of salvation we received. Jesus' blood bridged the gap between God and man, so where man had been thrown out of the Garden at one time, we again can have fellowship with our Creator. The tree of life, which was in the Garden, signified Jesus, and Cherubim (angels) guarded it day and night, but now that Jesus is our High Priest, we may approach the Throne of Grace with boldness. Thirdly, God cannot dwell where there is corruption in a church. In fact, He does not dwell in a church building at all. Christ is the church, and we are the people that make up His body. Remember what was said by Apostle Paul in Acts 17: 24? **"God who made the world and everything in it does not**

dwell in temples made with hands." *So you see, religion and God are completely different! We need to start looking for a relationship instead. Church can be anywhere a group of believers get together and worship God. Jesus and His disciples went from house to house, city to city, preaching the word. Another thing people do not understand is an idol of worship. Repeatedly, we feel that we need pictures and statues to look upon and pray. We even made Mary an idol of worship, and there are rosary beads to pray repetitious prayers so we can be forgiven of our sins, along with worshiping a dead man on the cross, even though He is risen and isn't there anymore. If you read the Ten Commandments by God in Exodus 20:4, you will understand what I mean.* "**Do not make an idol for yourself, whether it is in the shape of anything in the heavens above or on the earth below or in the waters under the earth.**"

This can be broken down quite easily. Man complicated it, not God. His word was pretty well direct. Let us even take angel worship. Why would we worship an angel, when Satan and his followers are angels themselves? A true angel knows the Word of God, and if he were sent by God to deliver you a message, why would he allow you to worship him? For that matter, why would you worship him when God says not too? When the angel appeared to John in Revelation 22:8, he wanted to fall down and worship the angel, but what did the angel say to him? "**Don't do that! I am a fellow slave with you, your brothers the prophet's and those who keep the words of this book. Worship God.**"

I find it strange when people create a god centered on the fundamentals of the Bible. It is as if we know not to kill someone, but we don't know how to worship God. The truth is, we get all this information from the same book, but interpret it differently. In time, after reading the word for so long and searching the truth, you would find that it's either black or white. There is no confusion with God if His Spirit leads you. Our thoughts are so primitive to God's way of thinking that we cannot comprehend His thought capacity. That is what aggravates man so much. He thinks that he has the answer, without realizing that God is the answer.

I have heard so many twisted doctrines that pervert the Word of God; that it drives me insane. It is actually sad to think that we can be smart about everything else in this world, except when it comes to the Bible. I heard one say to me at work that he believed Eve was not the first woman put on earth. Well, the truth is, according to the Bible, she was. So what doctrine came up with that idea? It was said in Genesis 2:21 that God caused a deep sleep to fall upon Adam and the woman was created from one of his ribs. It then goes on to say in Genesis 3:20, **"Adam named his wife Eve because she was the mother of all living."** It was apparent that the two were married, because 2:24 says, **"This is why a man leaves his father and mother and bonds with his wife, and they become one flesh."** I do not think Adam had a relationship other than with Eve, nor did he commit the act of adultery with another woman. I also don't think God took two ribs out of Adam to create another female for Adam to choose from. The truth is that another woman was never mentioned in Scripture. I also heard that Jesus had sexual relations with Mary. What an awful joke and blasphe-

mous thing to think! Jesus was God in the flesh as we talked about earlier in this book. He walked sinless to save the world from eternal damnation. Do you really think God allowed Himself to commit the act of adultery, when He was trying to fix what man had been messing up for all those years? Do you think that He would really break His own commandment, or for that matter, pick someone who would? Stop and think about it for a second. The only people who would believe such a foolish lie are the same that would deny Him as the Son of God. They acknowledge Him for being a good role model for religion and some great prophet who healed and performed miracles occasionally. In fact, God used those same people, along with the devil, to glorify Jesus once He rose from the dead! Humankind thought he had crucified Jesus with his own authority; when in reality, God allowed it to happen by His own authority. God has been in control since sin entered Eden. The joke was never on God, but everyone else including Satan. God, as usual, will take a bad situation and make it right for His own glory.

At anytime, God could have wiped out the world with His breath. Jesus would have never had to die if God fixed things from the start, but He had given us a free will. What kind of God would He have been if we were created perfect with no free will? We would have been running around like robots programmed to serve God. We do things for people because we want to, not because we have to. The only time we are forced to do something is when our bosses at work tell us to, and you know yourselves that it makes you feel like a slave. Yet we accept it, because money drives us to obedience. To sum it all up, would you enjoy worshiping God if you were forced to? Would He be God if His love for us were by way of force?

The New Age, as well as religion, has come up with ways to conform themselves without feeling guilty in whatever their practices are—sexual immorality or casting spells for gain (which includes rituals concerning money, power, and love). Even churches have created their own rules. I mean they keep the general laws, but throw in different twists to support a particular denomination. I have heard people telling me stuff like, "Well, you know, only Catholics will go to Heaven." It makes me laugh so much when I hear it presented like that. I am not just taking things out on a specific religion. I mean it as a whole. I can tell you, not once did Jesus ever say that only one denomination would enter into Heaven. God gave us the only solution to enter Heaven; it was to believe and receive the Lord Jesus as our Savior. That is it. Nothing can change that.

We need to keep our eyes focused on Jesus and His word to allow ourselves to not be led astray. Today pastors, as well as evangelists and prophets, can be just as guilty of such charges. Faith healers who travel around the world making money on false prophesy and healing the sick will be judged in that day. Making false accusations and promises that never happen are appalling, when one claims to be under the guidance of God. God said in Deuteronomy 18:19–20, "**I will hold accountable whoever does not listen to my words that he speaks in my name. But the prophet who dares to speak in My name a message I have not commanded him to speak, or speaks in the name of other gods, that prophet**

must die."

As we close the segment of this chapter, I have some encouraging words for the reader. If you are involved with certain beliefs and practices, know that it's never too late to turn your life around. You can pray to the Lord Jesus for repentance and forgiveness by asking Him into your life. He loves you enough to forgive you for whatever your past sins are. Renounce all involvement with the occult, all the sinful acts you have done, and you will be justified as Holy in His sight. It does not cost any money; just humble yourself before the Lord, and you will be saved. I'll bet if you were told that a thousand dollars would assure you eternal life that you would pay the amount—simply because you would feel that you were getting something in return for your payment. So why can't you think that eternal life is free? Why must you perform some act of works to feel better in your deeds? Maybe you have spent hundreds of dollars in consulting a psychic for your future. A psychic will only tell you what you want to hear. I do not have any doubt in my mind that some have a gift of second sight, but I assure you that it is contrary to God's command.

As we said earlier in this chapter, God forbids us to consult a divine answer from anyone other than Himself. Yes, you can resort to seeking familiar spirits for a particular answer or need, but it does not buy you life. There is always a price to pay when dealing with the occult or the black arts of magic. You cannot bribe God with anything; He is asking for true repentance. In all reality, religion and the New Age work hand in hand with one another to coexist together. Ever see those old cathedral churches?

When you look at the top of the building, what is some thing you may often see sitting up there? It would gargoyle statues. Of course, it is justified by not being an evil figure by people, simply because the church welcomes these images as protectors. Gargoyles were said to ward off evil. Most practicing witches usually possess these figures throughout their homes. As Christians, we are to rely on the Lord and His angels to keep us from harm. So why do we ask divine protection from such a demonic-looking beast? The answer is simple; false doctrine fits into our worldly way of thinking. If you read the Ten Commandments with us earlier, you would know that God said not to make carved images of any kind.

I once remember Pastor William Brown telling a story of an old church set in the Chicago area. I'm not sure of its name, but the small city had a huge cathedral building with four gargoyles on the roof protecting north, south, east, and west. The church stood high on a hill overlooking the city. You could even see it from the highway. Other pastors have told the man that he should not keep them up there as well, but he ignored their plea. Did you know during that particular year that the area surrounding the church had an increased rate of crime? I live two streets down from a Catholic church. Years ago some priests, who did not obey and respect their oaths as men of God, occupied it. One of them had left the church for reports of child molestation. A few years ago, we had an incredible lightning storm that hit us hard. Outside of a few trees damaging our electrical lines, lightning struck the church cross that stood high on its roof. The large cross fell and was found lying on the front lawn that morning. I am not trying to put down the Catholic Church, though it may seem that way. There are a lot of devout Christian's who attend masses weekly. I am simply stating, as to any Church organization, be careful and make sure God's Word receives honor with respect and accuracy.

Let us look at one more thing about the New Age movement—its paganistic holidays. Of course, the devil has to participate in such practices. Easter and Christmas are to name a few. Though we are not sure of the actual day, date, and time, we acknowledge the Lord's birth, death, and Resurrection on certain days of the year. The devil has his own scheme as well, and as I got older, I realized some interesting things. While Easter is celebrated for Jesus' Resurrection, a bunny rabbit that goes around giving us candy blinds us. While we celebrate Christmas for Jesus' birth, we have a man named Santa who flies around bringing us toys for being good throughout the year. He also was referred to as "Old Saint Nick." I have heard before that "Old Nick" was a name used to refer to the devil. I do not really know if there is any truth to that statement. However, I know one thing; if you unscrambled the name Santa, you will find it quite interesting (**Santa** - **Satan**).

The enemy found a way to blend into Jesus' days of celebration, convincing us that the two go hand in hand and are tied into each other—Jesus and Santa, Jesus and the rabbit. The devil has hi own holiday as well. We know it as Halloween. The correct term is "All Hollow's Eve." In paganism, as well as Satanism, it is considered to be the holiest night of the year. Witches honor it for different reasons than Satanists, but the two do share the same night for their celebration. Kids run around knocking on the *doors of their neighbors' houses, dressed in masks and filling their bags with all sorts of treats. Actually, it was said that witches wore masks on Halloween to ward off evil demonic spirits. Therefore, while everyone is getting candy and attending parties with their friends, the demonic realm is at an all time high. Halloween has an atmosphere all of its own. People love the fall—the leaves turning color, the comfortable weather, and the smell of its fresh air. It makes for a comfortable atmosphere. If you took a survey and asked people what is one of their favorite days of the year, you would be surprised to hear that a lot would say Halloween.*

In these end times, you will see that God is not playing around with his people, but neither are the forces of darkness. The time will come when you need to make a choice, or the decision will already be made for you. I pray that God will bless all who are dealing with this matter. I hope that whoever does read this will seek and find the Lord Jesus and discover the truth. Amen.

"In order to live the remaining time in the flesh, no longer for human desires, but for God's will. For there has already been enough time spent in doing the will of pagans: carrying on in unrestrained behavior, evil desires, drunkenness, orgies, carousing, and lawless idolatry."

-James 4:2–3

(9)
SATAN VS. MARRIAGE

This is probably the most difficult topic to discuss with anyone. I could write a whole book dealing with marriage all by itself, and we would not even get through a percentage of its true meaning. I'm going to touch ground on the basics of what a true marriage is and show you how Satan has blinded the world with lust, adultery, and, of course, divorce. This is one part of warfare that shows no mercy in this adulterous world.

First, you must understand that a covenant between husband and wife is meant to be eternal. Many of us understand marriage values to the extent of knowing our vows, but saying them is by far different than believing them. When two people are in love, they will promise each other everything and anything. Sometimes the newness of a relationship has more power than true love itself. We tend to mistake our lust and fleshly desires for what we think are love. The two are completely different and could be quite devastating to a household, if they are not under the covering of God.

A family that is under attack from the enemy will have stirred up some emotions and feelings that they never knew were there. It is such a complex style of warfare that it can take only a short time before a marriage can be destroyed. When we take our wedding vows at the altar, we are making an everlasting covenant before the eyes of the Lord. We vow to love and honor, in sickness and in health, until death we part. Unfortunately, most of the time, we leave those same vows at the altar and never hold them within our hearts.

God wanted us to follow certain rules and regulations before we get married. He wanted us to stay pure, remaining virgins until we found that special person to spend the rest of our lives with. He did not do it because He wanted us to be frustrated as virgins; He did it to save us from disaster. Of course, man did it his way and now the world is filled with disease. Think about it. If we followed God's plan with marriage, the world would be different. Let's take two scenarios and decide for ourselves which one we should have followed.

1. Godly marriage: We would have remained pure until the soul mates God put in our lives appeared. We also would have based our relationships strictly on family values. When we realized that they were the ones, then we would have thought about marriage, while remaining virgins. When that time came, we would have taken valued oaths to spend the rest of our lives with those people, totally under the guidance of God. We would have raised our families up, godly and morally, so our children would have learned as well. We would have stuck it out with our loved ones, because we would have valued the Word of God. There wouldn't have been worry about disease from out-of-marriage relationships, and our children would have stable, loving environments, secure in the knowledge that their parents' bond would be forever. Our families' problems would have been from the things in the world, not our

homes. *We would have all pulled together, making our families our top priorities. The covenant would have been sealed.*

2. Worldly marriage: We race to see how quickly we can lose our virginity—the younger the better. We get girls pregnant at young ages without taking responsibilities for our actions. We bounce from relationship to relationship, filling our voids due to prior relationships or marriages. We sleep with people we hardly know and engage in sexual immorality. We marry one, two, three times, as if it were nothing. We have children with each relationship in which we are involved. We develop diseases that cost us our lives and destroy our children's lives along the way. We justify the need to murder by having abortions. We get abused mentally and physically by partners, so we promote homosexuality because of our hate toward the opposite sex. We pay prostitutes to perform different acts of lust. We lie to our spouses, just to go out with our friends and lust after people we cannot have. The absence of a parent during school functions can be humiliating to our children, but we accept it as being normal. We never really think about how our kids feel about not having their mothers or fathers around school dances or sporting events. We say to our children, "Make sure you practice safe sex," instead of us telling them it's totally wrong until marriage.

It is sad to think how much we have lowered ourselves. Times will only get worse if we do not do something about it, but I'm afraid, my friends, that it's too late. Sex outside of true marriage has destroyed relationships, children, and lives. Do you know that the average marriage has a divorce rate within 1–3 years without children and 5–10 with children? That is nothing compared to a lifelong commitment that you took before the Lord. Therefore, I ask you this question, "Why did you marry?" If you stop and think of that question, you will probably come up with many answers. I'll bet you will find every reason for doing so, but not the one you needed to make your marriage last. Some say they did it for money, while others say they needed to get out of their parents' houses. Of course, we can't forget self-esteem. Some get married because they don't think much of themselves, so they cling onto the first person who shows them the attention they need. All reasons will not make a marriage last forever, and this is one way Satan can wipe out the entire world, if all else had failed—divorce, adultery, fornication, and sexual immorality.

Satan has corrupted relationships with God and man from the beginning of time. He was responsible for separating our relationships with God. He also deceived Eve, who then convinced Adam to eat of the fruit. She blamed the serpent, Adam blamed Eve, and we were divorced from God until Christ restored us again. Throughout the Bible, we see countless times how the enemy turned people against each other. Relationships are destroyed due to sin, jealousy, and deceit. Satan tried to attack Joseph, when he used Potipher's wife to seduce him. Even King David committed the act of adultery, when he fell into sin with Bathsheba. The enemy tried bringing fear to drive out the prophet, Elijah, from the land. He used King Ahab's adulterous wife, Jezebel, and she sent Elijah running to the hills seeking death. Every effective device Satan that used always had adultery or sexual perversion behind the motive.

As we know, man has killed man for the love of a woman. The power of love and sex has allowed the enemy to capitalize on weakness. Love will drive us to do just about anything to keep it. That is why Satan is so good at destroying marriages. If he has found a relationship based on the things that are not of God (materialistic happiness) then their marriage would be in jeopardy. The devil does, in fact, strike Christian marriages as well. If two believers are not walking according to their faith, they will eventually fall. How much easier do you think it is for him to destroy a marriage between two unbelievers?

Satan will take the weakest link in a marriage, work on its circumstances, and then execute. Satan will also take the spouse who has the most mixed-up emotions and twist them even more, by casting plenty of doubt so that the person feels like he or she deserves something or someone better. Satan is the master of deception, and will convince them that the grass is greener on the other side. I'm speaking about intense warfare far beyond your dreams when it comes to destroying the body of Christ. If there is no forgiveness or true love surrounding the marriage, it will fail.

I feel that this topic is the most painful to discuss. It affects our thoughts and willingness to function, unless some sort of restoration is made. Let's go deep with this topic and touch upon it at a different level. The devil will even use friends and influences that surround a specific marriage so that when sin enters into a home, it scatters like a plague, infecting all who are around it.

"The tongue is a restless evil, full of deadly

poison" as the Book of James, states in 3:8. The darts that fly at one another in a heated battle are relentless and the devil thrives on them. He lives for deceit and lies that can be mixed with truth. He will fill your minds with jealousy, anger, and rage, causing you to do something you would never think of doing. He will poison your thoughts by putting visual images of your spouse doing the unthinkable. He will drive you until your thoughts burn with fire. This all happens because the devil knows our weaknesses, our fleshly desires, and our passions for the need to love and feel affection. That is why friends and influences can play a major role in destroying a relationship. Sometimes the enemy will stir up an old friend or kindle an old flame from our past. That person could have been sent for one purpose only—to cause division. Remember, an unchecked bed of evil will only accelerate, never diminish.

See, it is good to have friends during times of chaos and tribulation, but you need to be careful of their motives. Maybe that person always had a crush on his friend and now is the perfect opportunity to strike. It may just be a crush on his friend's spouse and now he is only using her weakness for his gain. The enemy can use anything and anyone to bring about despair to a family. Close friends, counselors, priests, or pastors can all play a major role in destroying relationships. Maybe its jealousy or feelings that start to surface along the way. Sometimes, his intentions were not like that in the beginning, but as time went on, circumstances changed. A pastor is someone you can confide in, but a lonely damsel in distress can alter a dramatic change because of sin nature. Seduction and lust show no mercy.

I know some of you are saying to yourself, He's trying to tie in everyday life and circumstances, blaming it on the devil. *That may be true. You also may be thinking that I am giving you the philosophy on human nature. To an extent, I am, but I know the unseen aspect that comes into play as well. We become so caught up in man's imperfections that we fail to see the truth. How did we become this way? The answer is—sin.*

Our emotions are to love, hate, cry, and laugh. The sinful natures we possess lead us to kill or lie. It drives us to be deceptive, manipulating, cruel, and heartless, and that is where the enemy excels. God knows our free will and how much we can take. He knows how to push those simple emotions, such as love and hate. Animals kill for food, while man kills for gain, greed, and lust. These deadly sins exceed far beyond the fact that is caused by our species. We are too intelligent for that. Considering all this, I hope you can see how a marriage does not stand a chance without God. It is like taking all your sinful emotions and expecting two people of the opposite sex to live truly happily together for the rest of their lives. Even if you can sit and say to yourself, My marriage is fine without God, *then I would have to say you are totally blind, my friend.*

Your marriage can never be truly free if God is not in control. Some marriages are miserable ones, even though they may have a lot of money. Others have beauty, but still want more. Are the marriages based on love, health, and happiness are the ones that last? The relationships that have a biblical foundation and can communicate with one another are the ones that survive and can live through vicious storms.

Another problem that arises in a confused marriage is "Did I do the right thing? Is this the one for me?" If you have to second-guess yourself, then you may not really love that person. Many people are misguided when they are led by their emotions or by others cheering them on. Friends, if you were in sin before marriage and never repented or sought the Lord, then your marriage was doomed from the start. All you really succeeded in was prolonging the inevitable. A marriage built on sin, usually ends in sin, and we end up reaping what we sow. Even Christians can fall into their own desires, by being those who God never intended them to be with. They are under the assumption that because they are married that they are free from sin. Face it friends, two people who met on the terms of adultery will carry it over to their next marriage. Did you know that if one commits adultery and remarries again, he or she is an adulterer for the rest of his or her life? If you read the Book of Romans, starting at Chapter 7:2, it will explain.

"By law a married woman is bound to her husband as long as he is alive, but if her husband dies, she is released from the law of marriage. So then, if she marries another man while her husband is still alive, she is called an adulterous."

The Law of Moses stated that if one commits adultery, his or her spouse can get a certificate of divorce and be permitted to remarry. Except for adultery and death, one is bound to his or her marriage for life. Anything short of that is a sin in the eyes of God, unless one repents. It is like a domino effect that plagues the world with lust and sexual immoral-

ity. That is why the divorce rate is so high today; sin has corrupted purity. Even if you think you are off the hook just because you never have been married before, well, you are wrong. Unless you have never had sexual relations with anyone, you still fall into the category of fornication. That is when two people engage in physical relations outside of marriage, which can be carried over to your first marriage as defilement.

Let us now look at the godly side of a blessed marriage, one who is dealing with warfare. That means two people are walking in God's plan and are encountering strong, demonic attack. First, you need to know that the devil wants to break up all Christian marriages. The best way to destroy the body of Christ is to divide it. It states in Ephesians 5:25, "Husbands are to love their wives just as Christ loved the church and gave himself up for her." Marriages between two believers are an incredible bond that God does not want destroyed. We are supposed to become one flesh with our spouses. There are some questions concerning man's position as the authority in a relationship, but not the way some husbands may feel about it. Some husbands abuse the power of Scripture, when it says wives are supposed to submit themselves to their husbands. Just because Scripture says men are supposed to rule over their wives, it does not mean it in an abusive sense. Wives were said to have been the weaker vessels, but their jobs are just as important. Iron may be stronger than wool, but the two are just as valuable. Men are to be the heads of the households in more of a spiritual aspect, a royal priesthood as the Bible states. When concerning Christian values and decisions, the man should *be more accountable, since he is the spiritual leader of his family. It does not mean to abuse the position he has by treating his spouse as the lower being. That is how the enemy works on destroying a family, by keeping a wife's self-esteem at an all time low. It will only cause deep emotional pain and anger, until the wife either divorces her husband or goes and seeks to have an adulterous relationship with someone.*

Many times the cheating spouse will have an affair with another Christian. It could be with some-body at his or her church or through a friend. They end up believing that God made a way of escape for them by meeting someone else just as their lives were about to get worse. That is only another deception of the enemy, to leak more sin into a Christian's life and cause more pain within the body of Christ. Remember what Jesus had said in Matthew 19:5–6, when He talked about marriage, **"For this reason a man will leave his father and mother and be united to his wife, and the two will become one flesh. So they are no longer two, but one. Therefore what God has joined together, let not man separate."**

God does not want us to divorce one another. We are to value our marriages and enjoy our spouses all the days of our lives. We sometimes tend to allow our children to get involved with the decisions we make as well. I have heard many times from couples that their children control a marriage by siding with a certain parent. One may put their children before his or her spouse and that can be another way for the enemy to operate in warfare. Now I am not saying we are not to love our children and think the world of them. I, too, have children whom I love very much, and if they were in danger in any way, I would heed to their voices. I am talking about manipulation that can cause division in a marriage. Remember, before our children were our spouses, and after our children grow up, it will still end up being our spouses. A wife or husband is someone we are to love until death. Except for an ungodly act, we are to side with our spouse over anyone and anything that can come between our marriages.

I hope you have a better understanding of how the enemy works in a marriage. There is so much to discuss; we would never have enough time to confer on everything. There are many books written by Christian authors that deal with marriage. You can use them for resources. I will end this chapter with four simple guidelines to follow in building a strong foundation to a long-lasting marriage. May the Lord bless your marriage and keep it blazing with love and forgiveness. Understand that Satan does not want your marriage blessed and will stop at nothing to destroy it.

1. Communication (Always take a few minutes out of each day to talk to one another.)
2. Trust and honesty (Never be afraid to tell each other everything, no matter how serious it may be.)
3. Spend time in prayer (Take time out to pray together daily, outside of your own individual prayer life.)
4. Choose friends wisely (Trust your friends; make sure they are Spirit-filled believers.)

"I hate divorce, says the Lord God of Israel, and I hate a man's covering himself with violence as well as with his garment, says the Lord Almighty. So guard yourself in your spirit, and do not break faith.*"*

-Malachi 2:16

(10)
SATAN VS. DEATH

This is one of the most controversial top-ics of them all. It deals with life after death. Of course, what makes this topic so volatile is the fact that death is final here on earth. No one has been gone long enough to come back with anything con-crete. Meaning, outside of near-death experiences or someone who was revived minutes later, no one has passed on for a few years and come back with the assurance of what really goes on the other side. You hear of many opinions, whether it is reincarnation or the fact that there is nothing at all on the other side. Some people think that the Bible was created as a guideline to a better life and a good way to accept death. We are now going to touch ground on the life after this world, whether it is a physical and spiritual death or life eternally in Christ Jesus.

*First, you need to realize that we, as humans, are made up of body, soul, and spirit. Therefore, our flesh decays in the ground after we pass, but our spirit carries on. Jesus said something very interest-ing in the Book of Matthew (10:28). He said, "**Do not be afraid of those who kill the body but cannot kill the soul. Rather, be afraid of the One who can destroy both soul and body in hell.***" The enemy has worked major warfare in convincing man that death is nothing like the Bible states, and of course, why would he?*

The enemy has tried to corrupt man with so many illusions on the topic of death. Some believe that we go nowhere when we pass on, while others believe that we return here with a different body. Others create their own interpretations of what they think Heaven and hell are like, while others believe that there is no hell. Some even believe that earth is hell and when we die, we go to Heaven. The devil does not want us to believe in hell, because if we did, we would surely have second thoughts as to where we would choose to go. I can say to you, friends— this world is not hell by a long shot.

Hell was designed and created for the devil and his angels. God never intended for anyone else to be there. It is by our free will and the decisions we make that decide our eternal future. You see, when we are born as an infant, we are unaware of what sin really is. When we reach the age of knowing right from wrong and good from evil—we become accountable to face judgment. I hear a lot of people say, "I'm a good person; I don't hurt anyone. Why would I go to hell?"

You may truly be a good person. You might have a good heart, you might be giving, and you might attend church every week, yet that does not mean you are going to Heaven. The only way to get to Heaven is by receiving Jesus into our hearts. That is it. If people want to enter Heaven, they will do what is required of them. No good work will get you there. We are born into sin, we are aware of sin, we commit sin, and we will die in sin without Christ. The only way to go to Heaven is to be sinless and perfect as our Lord Jesus, and that will never happen. You could have said that you only sinned a few *times in your life (which is highly improbable), done a thousand good things, and yet it still would not be enough. Only Jesus can cleanse you from all unrighteousness.*

Hell is a place of torment, where your being is totally separated from God forever. It is also a continuous pain and reminder of the former things we have done to get us there in the first place—guilt, pain, and suffering beyond comprehension. People ask me all the time, "How could your spirit burn if you are already dead?" Though that sounds true, there is an answer. A friend awhile back gave me a good description of it. When the angel of the Lord appeared to Moses at the burning bush, you will notice that the bush was burning, but it was not being consumed. Hell works the same way; spirits and souls burn, but they are not consumed. Let us look at a story that Jesus told about the rich man and Lazarus in Luke 16:22–26, then we will break it down.

"The time came when the beggar died and the angels carried him to Abraham's side. The rich man also died and was buried in hell, where he was in torment. He looked up and saw Abraham far away, with Lazarus by his side. So he called to him, 'Father Abraham, have pity on me and send Lazarus to dip the tip of his finger in water and cool my tongue, because I am in agony because of this fire.' But Abraham replied 'Son, remember in your lifetime you received your good things, but now he is comforted here and you are in agony. And besides all this, between us and you a chasm has been fixed, so that those who want to go from here to you cannot, nor can anyone cross

over from there to us.' "

A lot can come from this story Jesus told. A few different questions can be answered concerning death. First, Jesus Himself gave us concrete information about hell. So His words are of higher value than some theory man may have. Let's do some Scripture breakdown. It will open new horizons for your mind to ponder.

1. The beggar died and was carried off by the angels. We learned that when we die as believers, angels escort us to Heaven.

2. The rich man died and was buried. We see that the rich man died without God, and as a result, he was left alone.

3. Hell is a place of torment. We see that hell is an actual place of torment, a place where unbelievers end up immediately after they die. The Greek word for hell is also referred to as **hades.**

4. The beggar was taken to Abraham's side. We learn there is a place of rest for believers. In the King James' version, it is translated as Abraham's bosom, which means paradise. There is also the theory that paradise resides in the third Heaven, where it is believed also that Jesus and the other members of the Trinity dwell. Just before Jesus died on the cross, he said to the thief, **"Today is the day when you will be with me in paradise."**

5. He looked up and saw Abraham far away. This proves that we are conscious of our surroundings and also are able to identify other people around us.

6. I am in agony because of this fire. This clearly states that we can physically feel pain and torment. Jesus had also said that hell was a place where there would be wailing and gnashing of teeth. Seems to me like a place where we can feel every bit of suffering a soul has to offer.

7. A chasm is fixed that cannot be passed. This says a lot about life after death. Taking the two who died in this Scripture, though they ended up in different places, they ended up somewhere. Though being in hell, the rich man could not pass to Abraham's bosom, and likewise, the beggar could not pass as well. So if two people ended up somewhere, believer or nonbeliever, they still could not return. If you read on into the next passage, you will also find that the rich man had asked Abraham to allow him to go back and warn his family about hell, but his request was denied. See friends, once you have passed on, the decision has already made for you, by you.

There is no proof as to spirits roaming the earth once they have passed on. We can watch all sorts of TV shows on ghost sightings, but the fact remains the same, the evidence is no greater than the biblical views on death. It is easy to say people are gifted in speaking to the dead. Man can do a multitude of things when it comes to making money. They can glorify death and make it appear so fascinating that we can all become intrigued by their interpretations. Ask yourself this question, and think about it for a moment. *If one claims to have seen a loved one who had passed on, wouldn't he describe his or her appearance the way he or she was last seen?* Meaning, you hear all sorts of stories about someone encountering a ghost, say a late uncle. They usually describe them wearing a checkered shirt or a baseball cap. The thing that gets me is this: How could they have been wearing certain apparel from long ago, when the last thing they were seen in was what he or she wore at their funeral? It's so easy to deceive people, especially if one has a gift for marketing a specific product. Remember, friends, in the entertainment world, the media, and in music, death sells.

I do not doubt that these mediums and fortunetellers have a special insight into the unknown world, because they do. I can also say that if God does not send them, they are of the dark realm. I believe according to God's laws and commands that these mediums receive information from "familiar spirits." It occurs when a certain spirit is able to feed on a person's insight about someone who had passed on. These spirits can also familiarize them with loved ones, so that they believe they are actually speaking to relatives on the other side. The illusion and motive for these spirits generating you information is for one purpose only, to gain your trust for something bigger. See, if they can convince you that the other side is different, then there is no need for God and the Bible. They will lead you to believe that ghosts are seen running around in houses, reuniting with loved ones, they even throw pets into the picture. All is deception. Remember earlier when we talked about Satan being transformed into an angel of light? Well, this is how he operates, people, blinding the world to the stone cold truth—hell.

Hell is not a party for friends to reunite and have a good time. It is not about an eternal party that never ends. If people only knew of hell's reality, they would not crack jokes while they were still alive. It only takes a bizarre or freak accident to condemn a soul to an eternity of long-suffering. I pray that it will not be you.

Satan and his angels will burn in the lake of fire, as well as the sinners who never repented for their sins, because they never chose Christ. Right now people, as well as certain angels, are awaiting judgment as we speak. The lake of fire has not been opened yet; the worst degree hasn't been unleashed at this point. That is why Satan has nothing too lose by getting your soul. His desire is to take down as many as he can, while he can.

It's the devil who comes to kill, steal, and destroy, not God. In the Book of Job, you will see that Satan had the ability to go before the Lord. He had to get permission from God concerning what to do and what not to do when it came to God's children. God does allow us to go through hard times, with the hope that we come out of it stronger and wiser. Sometimes it is to build our faith, while other times it has to teach us a lesson. Satan said to God in (KJV) Job 1: 10; *"**Hast not thou made a hedge about him, and about his house, and about all that he hath on every side?**"* See! God protects us and has the final say, but it still comes down to our obedience. God gives permission for things to happen, but it is sin and Satan that cause the actual occurrence of accidents, sickness, disease, and death.

I know that it is hard to understand certain things about life's mysteries. I lost a few friends in the Station nightclub fire and new some of the survivors who were badly injured. One of the friends I lost was in my house watching a movie just a few weeks prior to the incident. I was tremendously devastated and wondered why this had to happen. Situations like these never can be understood. I will say that survivors who escape a life and death situations should count them as blessings.

Know that it was not by luck or chance that you survived, but by a divine purpose for which you were called. Do you heed to that calling? It seems that death has a design for all of us, but realize this, death also has a Master to bow down to. His name is Jesus.

See, friends, God is not to blame for tragic events. Though we would like to blame Him, there are still some things that can't be answered as to why. One day it will all make sense, and all our questions will be answered. Sometimes God will allow someone to be taken earlier, knowing that his or her life would have been much more difficult had he or she survived birth. I have no doubt at all that the unborn, as well as infants, are not expected to give an account, but will go straight to Heaven when they pass away. God knew us before we were born, and He does not forget anyone of us. When Cain killed Able, what did God say to Cain in Genesis 4:11? *"Thy brother's blood crieth unto me from the ground."* The (KJV) Book of Jeremiah (1:5) states, *"Before I formed thee in the belly I knew thee."* God loves all of us, and though He is forgiving, He's still a God of justice.

There is so much more to speak of and learn concerning death that we would not resolve anything without getting into some debate or argument. There are countless numbers of stories of those who have had near death experiences, but that's just it, they were near, not permanent. We will go somewhere when we die, and we will also be judged, based upon the life we led. Everyone and everything has an order to follow, and we will always have to answer to a higher authority as well. Whatever we had gotten away with while on earth will one day have to be accounted and answered for when God asks. Heaven is a beautiful place God has created for us, but only we can decide if we will ever get there. If you do not believe in the God of the Bible and His requests, then you will have your reward here and now. However, know that your existence here comes with a price, whether you like it or not. My prayer is that all of your names will be written in the Lamb's Book of Life, and you will be rewarded eternally for your decision while still alive. It is not too late to change your ways now, but it must occur here, while still alive in this body. I have always simplified the theory of God and His word by something I tell many people when they ask me, "Well, how do you know the Bible is actually true?"

I simply say, "If you do all of God's requirements and there is no Heaven, then you had nothing to lose." You lived life holy, caring, forgiving, and with many great morals. However, if there is, and you didn't repent, then you will suffer eternal damnation for your own selfish ignorance, with no one to blame except you. As your soul is burning in a never-ending lake of fire and brimstone, as you are screaming for help, you will remember this conversation, and know that I tried. I tried to be the last voice you may have heard about the truth, before it was too late."

"And death and hell were cast into the lake of fire. This was the second death. And whoever was not found written in the book of life was cast into the lake of fire." - Revelation 20:14–15

EPILOGUE

I hope that you have enjoyed yourselves while reading this book. I wanted to educate you on some areas that are usually overlooked. It has been my pleasure to share with you some things that I hold so dear to my heart. I pray that all of you find and seek the truth about God. Only through the blood of Jesus Christ, can we have redemption and inherit eternal life. I also feel it is important to understand that God is alive and waiting for you to call to Him. Life does not have to be boring, while waiting to pass on to the next life. It is always exciting with God; He will never cease to amaze you in all that He does.

Spiritual warfare is no joke. It plays a major role in our lives daily, and most of us cannot detect it because we are too concerned with the things that are seen with our natural eyes. I hope to have helped in assisting you to want to reach further and search the deep acts of God. Being a spiritual warrior means to step up and do the job, nobody seems to want a part of. We don't do it for money or greed; we do it because we have a passion to serve God and to see all have a chance to inherit true happiness. Do not be a closet Christian. Don't let the devil strip away what God has freely given. Some Christians are meek and mild, worrying about themselves, and in the process, edifying only themselves. They become far too fragile to do the work that the Lord asks them to do. Be in the trenches of battle, because whether you fight or not, the enemy and his forces are still going to come at you.

David said in Psalm 23, *"Though I walk through the valley of the shadow of death, I will fear no evil."* See, David said though I walk, not walked. We are always going to walk; it never ends until the work is finished. If we fall and we will, let's get up and march on. Satan wants to rob us of all the things that God wants us to have. He will use strategies of all kinds to block the flow of developing spiritual growth. When I saw the movie The *Passion of the Christ* I realized just how much God loves us that He would allow His Son to suffer beyond belief, in order to free the world from eternal death. I mentioned in my introduction that I would be happy to be a light in the world for just one person to turn aside from his ways and reach out to God. Now that I have finished, I pray to God that everyone would be blessed and turn to Jesus Christ, the Son of the living God.

If you never had the opportunity to accept Jesus into your life and believe that you are ready, then I would love to lead you into prayer. Just pray with me and receive Him into your hearts. There is no better time than the present. We don't know what tomorrow brings, and I don't want you to miss this chance. So just pray a few simple words with me and receive the gift of eternal life. Are you ready? Let's do it together.

"Lord Jesus, I am a sinner. I have lived my life according to my will, and though it may have gained me happiness, it will not gain me eternal life in your kingdom. I ask you, Lord Jesus, to come into my life and be my Lord and Savior. I ask you

to forgive me of my sins and cleanse me from all unrighteousness. I believe that you died on my behalf and rose again and took the keys of death and Hades, so I would not have to be punished for the sins I committed. I know you are seated at the right hand of the Father in your wonderful kingdom. I, too, want to be apart of everlasting life. I receive you into my heart, Lord. Come and live with me forever, Amen."

If you just prayed that with me, Amen! Welcome to God's kingdom, my friend. You are now a child of light, and your name is now written in the Lamb's Book of Life for eternity. Death has no power over you from this day forward. Your walk may be difficult at times, but know that Jesus overcame the world. Now you have the Holy Spirit within you, to help you, teach you, and guide you into all truth. I pray that the Lord blesses you and keeps you well. I also recommend you to find a good church to attend. There you will meet other Christian's so that your faith will strengthen. I suggest that you take it slow by reading the Bible a few minutes a day. Ask the Holy Spirit to help you increase and develop your prayer life. Before you know it, you will have a close and intimate relationship with the Master of the universe—God. It is also important to understand that going to church and Bible studies are a big part of being a Christian, but there is more to God than just that. It requires fellowship and communication with the Lord. Spend time in the presence of the Lord daily. Find a special place to pray, and your Father who sees in secret, will reward you openly. Jesus is alive! His desire is to know you and be a part of your life forever.

Again, I want to thank you for listening and giving me the chance to share with you the Good News about Jesus. Keep your eyes focused on Jesus and the truth; enjoy your Christian walk. I hope to meet with you all one day, where we can rejoice in Heaven together. I hope that you pursue a solid walk with your new life in Christ Jesus our Lord, and never stop moving forward. Sometimes we may find ourselves losing the fight! However, the battle is already won. May the Lord bless you and keep you safe from all evil, in Jesus' name, Amen.

"But he was wounded for our transgressions; he was bruised for our iniquities: The chastisement of our peace was upon him; and with his strips we are healed." *- Isaiah 53:5*

SCRIPTURE INDEX

Contact Joe Cetrone or order more
copies of this book at

TATE PUBLISHING, LLC

127 East Trade Centre Terrace
Mustang, Oklahoma 73064

(888) 361 - 9473

Tate Publishing, LLC

www.tatepublishing.com